Daily

GRADE 6

Language

Review

Skills Scope & Sequence

Reading Comprehension

Skill	W1	W2	W3	W4	W5	W6	W7	W8	W9	W10	W11	W12	W13	W14	W15	W16	W17	W18	W19	W20	W21	W22	W23	W24	W25	W26	W27	W28	W29	W30	W31	W32	W33	W34	W35	W36
Analogies	X			X	X		X	X			X	X		X		X		X		X				X	X			X					X		X	
Categorizing			X			X	X	X			X				X				X			X				X						X	X	X	X	
Cause and Effect			X		X						X					X				X	X				X	X			X		X					
Fact/Opinion		X	X					X		X		X	X				X	X			X		X		X			X		X	X		X		X	
Fiction/Nonfiction						X				X						X					X															
Idioms			X		X					X			X							X				X	X				X		X		X		X	
Figurative Language		X					X			X					X					X				X					X			X				X
Inference	X			X															X		X					X					X	X		X		

Vocabulary/Word Study

Skill	W1	W2	W3	W4	W5	W6	W7	W8	W9	W10	W11	W12	W13	W14	W15	W16	W17	W18	W19	W20	W21	W22	W23	W24	W25	W26	W27	W28	W29	W30	W31	W32	W33	W34	W35	W36
Base Words/Prefix/Suffix	X	X	X			X	X		X		X			X	X	X			X		X	X			X		X	X					X	X	X	X
Contractions			X	X	X	X		X					X				X			X	X					X							X			
Homophones	X	X	X	X	X	X	X	X	X	X	X	X	X	X	X	X	X	X	X	X	X	X	X	X	X	X	X	X	X	X	X	X	X	X	X	X
Synonyms/Antonyms	X	X	X	X	X	X		X			X	X	X		X		X	X			X	X	X	X		X				X	X	X			X	X
Word Meaning from Context		X				X		X				X		X			X		X		X	X			X			X					X	X		
Spelling	X	X	X	X	X	X	X	X	X	X	X	X	X	X	X	X	X	X	X	X	X	X	X	X	X	X	X	X	X	X	X	X	X	X	X	X
Phonics		X																			X															

Punctuation

Skill	W1	W2	W3	W4	W5	W6	W7	W8	W9	W10	W11	W12	W13	W14	W15	W16	W17	W18	W19	W20	W21	W22	W23	W24	W25	W26	W27	W28	W29	W30	W31	W32	W33	W34	W35	W36
Punctuation — End of Sentence	X	X	X	X	X	X	X	X	X	X	X	X	X	X	X	X	X	X	X	X	X	X	X	X	X	X	X	X	X	X	X	X	X	X	X	X
Periods — Abbreviations/Initials	X	X	X	X	X	X			X	X	X	X			X	X			X	X	X	X	X			X	X	X	X			X	X	X		X
Underline — Magazines, Books, Plays				X			X											X												X	X	X				X
Run-on Sentences		X										X											X			X								X	X	X
Quotation Marks in Speech		X	X		X	X	X	X		X	X	X	X		X	X		X	X	X	X	X		X			X	X	X	X	X		X		X	X
Quotation Marks — Songs, Poems, Short Stories				X									X	X						X				X			X		X							
Commas in a Series			X		X	X	X	X			X		X			X	X	X		X	X	X		X	X	X			X		X	X	X	X		
Commas in Dates/Addresses					X	X		X				X	X				X									X			X		X	X		X		
Comma to Separate Dialogue		X	X		X	X		X		X		X	X			X	X	X	X	X	X			X			X	X	X	X		X			X	X
Commas in Direct Address/Interjection					X						X					X				X			X					X					X	X		
Commas in Compound Sentences	X						X	X	X	X								X				X		X				X		X			X	X	X	
Commas After an Introductory Phrase/Clause	X				X	X	X		X	X						X		X		X	X	X	X	X	X	X		X		X		X		X		X
Commas with Nonrestrictive Appositive			X											X						X			X					X		X	X		X			
Apostrophes in Contractions	X	X	X	X	X	X			X	X	X	X	X			X	X			X	X	X	X	X	X			X	X				X		X	X
Apostrophes in Possessives	X	X	X	X			X	X	X			X	X	X	X			X	X	X			X	X			X	X	X	X	X				X	X

Capitalization

Skill	W1	W2	W3	W4	W5	W6	W7	W8	W9	W10	W11	W12	W13	W14	W15	W16	W17	W18	W19	W20	W21	W22	W23	W24	W25	W26	W27	W28	W29	W30	W31	W32	W33	W34	W35	W36
Beginning of Sentence	X	X	X	X	X	X	X	X	X	X	X	X	X	X	X	X	X	X	X	X	X	X	X	X	X	X	X	X	X	X	X	X	X	X	X	X
Days/Months/Holidays		X		X	X	X					X	X							X	X		X	X			X						X			X	
Books/Songs/Poems				X				X					X	X			X			X	X		X			X		X		X	X		X			
Proper Names/Titles of People	X	X	X	X	X	X	X	X	X	X	X	X	X	X	X	X	X	X	X	X	X	X	X	X	X	X	X	X	X	X	X	X	X	X	X	X
Names of Places	X		X		X	X				X	X	X	X	X	X				X	X	X	X	X	X	X	X	X	X	X	X					X	X

Grammar & Usage

Skill	W1	W2	W3	W4	W5	W6	W7	W8	W9	W10	W11	W12	W13	W14	W15	W16	W17	W18	W19	W20	W21	W22	W23	W24	W25	W26	W27	W28	W29	W30	W31	W32	W33	W34	W35	W36
Correct Article/Adjective/Adverb											X					X						X						X	X			X	X			
Types of Adjectives/Adverbs				X	X											X			X	X		X	X			X			X			X				
Singular/Plural Nouns	X		X				X			X		X			X	X	X	X	X	X	X	X	X			X		X		X		X	X			
Subject/Object Pronouns		X		X			X	X	X				X	X		X		X			X			X			X	X	X			X	X	X		X
Possessive Nouns				X													X	X				X	X	X					X							
Common/Proper Nouns											X	X				X	X						X		X			X				X				X
Verb Forms	X		X	X	X			X	X	X	X	X	X	X	X	X	X	X	X	X	X	X	X	X	X	X			X	X	X	X	X	X	X	X
Verb Tense			X	X	X	X				X					X	X	X	X		X		X		X			X	X		X					X	
Subject/Predicate						X				X			X	X			X			X	X		X			X	X	X	X		X		X		X	
Parts of Speech		X		X	X		X	X	X				X	X	X	X	X	X			X		X			X	X	X	X	X	X	X		X	X	
Comparative/Superlative	X	X								X	X				X	X			X					X	X	X	X			X	X				X	X
Subject/Verb Agreement			X	X	X			X	X	X	X	X	X	X	X	X	X				X	X		X	X	X	X			X	X	X	X	X	X	X
Sentence Types	X				X					X						X		X	X										X							X
Double Negatives	X	X			X								X																							
Sentence Combination				X					X					X					X				X													

Reference Skills

Skill	W1	W2	W3	W4	W5	W6	W7	W8	W9	W10	W11	W12	W13	W14	W15	W16	W17	W18	W19	W20	W21	W22	W23	W24	W25	W26	W27	W28	W29	W30	W31	W32	W33	W34	W35	W36
Alphabetical Order		X		X			X		X								X		X					X						X			X			
Dictionary Guide Words	X								X						X	X		X			X		X							X			X		X	
Reference Materials			X										X			X				X					X											
Syllabication		X				X	X		X		X			X			X				X			X					X	X				X	X	X

How to Use *Daily Language Review*

This book is divided into 36 weekly sections.
Each weekly unit provides daily assessment activities.

Monday through Thursday

- Students edit sentences and make corrections to punctuation, capitalization, and grammar.

- Students complete items that practice a variety of language and reading skills.

Friday

- Students focus on practicing a single skill.

- Students complete a daily progress record that tracks their work for the week.

Hints and Suggestions

Customize the daily review lessons to meet the needs of your class.

- Look ahead each week at the skills being practiced. If you encounter a new skill, complete the item as a class.

- Correct students' work together to model the correct responses.

- As skills are repeated throughout the year, monitor students' mastery.

Correct these sentences.

1. duz his cuzin lives in unother sity

_____

2. After james and tim cleened the garage grandma gave them five dollars

_____

Singular or plural?

3. cattle _____

Circle the word in each row that is spelled correctly.

4. oxigun   oxegun   oxygen

5. umpare   umpire   umpyre

Write an antonym for each word.

1. demolish _____

2. imaginary _____

Correct these sentences.

3. the Childrens valubles were storeed in the teachers closit

_____

4. that Hot Rod is the noisier vehicul on my Block

_____

Declarative, interrogative, imperative, or exclamatory?

5. Who's your favorite music artist? _____

WEEK 1

Wednesday

Name: _____

Correct these sentences.

1. wernt their no milk in the refrijerator

_____

2. there going to come to sea me at 7 pm

_____

Choose the best word to complete this analogy.

3. heavy : light :: near : _____

   close   far   next door   traveled

Where would the following probably take place?

4. The boy watched from the terminal as the commuter plane landed on the runway.

_____

Write the root or base word.

5. illogical _____

WEEK 1

Thursday

Name: _____

Write the correct abbreviation.

1. Avenue _____

2. pound _____

What print reference source would you use to find the meaning of *thesaurus*?

3. _____

Correct these sentences.

4. lets play a game of Soccor to day

_____

5. antonio was to big for his bike sew he sold it at red barn flee market

_____

WEEK 1 Friday

Name: _____

Use the comparative or the superlative form of the word in parentheses to complete each sentence.

1. (tall)   Suzi was the _____ player on the basketball team.

2. (heavy) Mark is _____ than Steve.

3. (hard)   This is the _____ homework I've had all year.

4. (busy)   Every Saturday morning, the mall is the _____ place in town.

5. (long)   Most snakes are _____ than worms.

WEEK 1 My Progress

Name: _____

How many did you get correct each day? Color the squares.

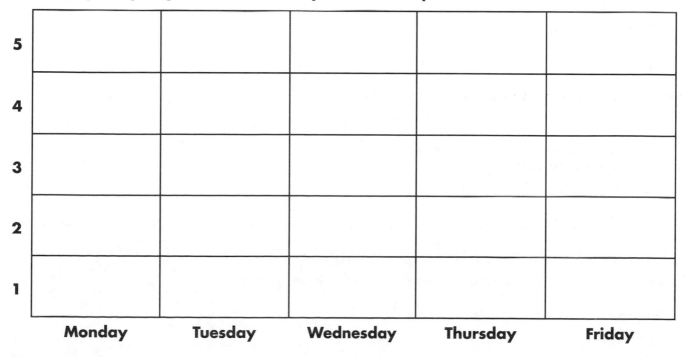

	Monday	Tuesday	Wednesday	Thursday	Friday
5					
4					
3					
2					
1					

Correct these sentences.

1. my Dad gave the prezint two pete and I

_____

2. it werent no serprize I new he wood do it

_____

Use context clues to determine the meaning of the bolded word.

3. The timeline gave the events in **chronological** order.

_____

Fact or opinion?

4. Over 75 percent of the students had a library card. _____

5. Every student should read one book each month. _____

Write a synonym for *succeeded*.

1. _____

Circle the word that comes first in alphabetical order.

2. fiber   feverish   festive   fervor   fertilize

Correct these sentences.

3. aprul is my faverutest month of the year

_____

4. we mayd the last paiment on hour new computor

_____

Write the pronoun that would replace the underlined nouns.

5. <u>Bernie</u> and <u>Ben</u> went orienteering with the Scouts. _____

WEEK
2 **Wednesday** Name:

Correct these sentences.

1. the work men layed a straite track for the frayt train

_____

2. maggie claymd she wuz to busy to dew her home work

_____

Name this part of a friendly letter.

3. Your pen pal, _____

Simile or metaphor?

4. The butterfly was as graceful as a ballerina. _____

Circle the adverb in this sentence.

5. Touch the new puppy gently so you don't injure it.

WEEK
2 **Thursday** Name:

Circle the word that comes last in alphabetical order.

1. shale   shaft   shady   shallot   shaky

How many syllables does this word have?

2. relationship _____

Correct these sentences.

3. mrs peters asked mr beckman will the concert start at 700 or 730

_____

4. the workmen has come to fix the oven in sammys kitchin

_____

Complete the word to make the /l/ sound.

5. sever _____

WEEK 2 Friday

Name: _____

Add a suffix to each of these words to answer the clue.

1. One who studies plants and animals   biolog _____

2. Not taking care as you work   care _____

3. One who does not tell the truth   li _____

4. In an unusual manner   strange _____

5. Being filled with a feeling of joy   joy _____

WEEK 2 My Progress

Name: _____

How many did you get correct each day? Color the squares.

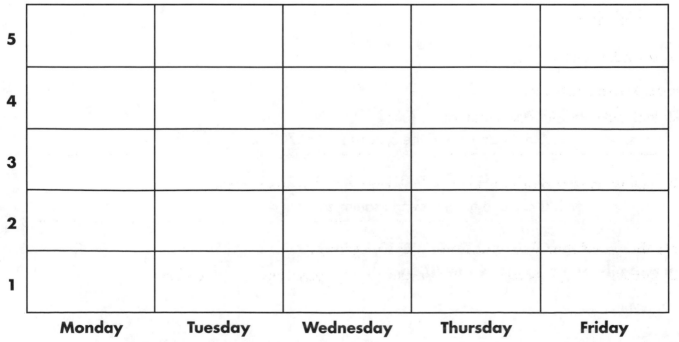

	Monday	Tuesday	Wednesday	Thursday	Friday
5					
4					
3					
2					
1					

WEEK 3 **Monday**

Name: _____

Correct these sentences.

1. we had a flat tire amos wuz sun burned and we got losted

   _____

2. chris thought I hope thay will chose me for there teem

   _____

Circle the correct abbreviation for *Doctor*.

3. Doc   Dr   Dr.   none of these

Write the correct salutation for a business letter to the doctor, Ben Corliss.

4. _____

Write the meaning of this idiom.

5. Winning the race was quite <u>a feather in my cap.</u>

   _____

© Evan-Moor Corp. • Daily Language Review • EMC 576

WEEK 3 **Tuesday**

Name: _____

Synonyms or antonyms?

1. arrival, departure   _____

2. abandon, discontinue   _____

Correct these sentences.

3. look out below he called that rock is falling

   _____

4. mother and her polish friend mrs. slovik went to a chinese resterant

   _____

Circle the word that does not belong in this group.

5. granite   quartz   feldspar   gasoline   amber

© Evan-Moor Corp. • Daily Language Review • EMC 576

Name:

Correct these sentences.

1. my friend mr. murphy visited churchs in canada china and japan

_____

2. there mom ask them to go to blacks market for her

_____

Circle the cause and underline the effect.

3. The campers had to be rescued after they wandered off the trail and became lost.

Singular or plural?

4. phenomena _____

Write the past tense of the verb _teach_.

5. _____

Name:

Write the contraction that is made from these two words.

1. will not _____

What print reference source would you use to find several synonyms for _walked_?

2. _____

Correct these sentences.

3. why due I have to due my home work now asked tori

_____

4. its best to get you're work done before you watch tv said mom

_____

Rewrite this word, adding a prefix.

5. appoint _____

© Evan-Moor Corp. • Daily Language Review • EMC 576

WEEK 3 · Friday

Name: _____

Read the following paragraph and decide if the underlined parts have a capitalization error, a punctuation error, a spelling error, or no error.

<u>Ancient Egypt a rich and prosperous nation</u> depended on farming. <u>The crops growen by farmers</u>
        1   **2**

living <u>in the nile valley</u> fed and clothed Egypt's people. Farmers <u>raised cattle geese oxen and</u>
              3   **4**

<u>pigs.</u> They planted wheat, flax, and a variety of fruits and vegetables.
    5

1. _____

2. _____

3. _____

4. _____

5. _____

WEEK 3 · My Progress

Name: _____

How many did you get correct each day? Color the squares.

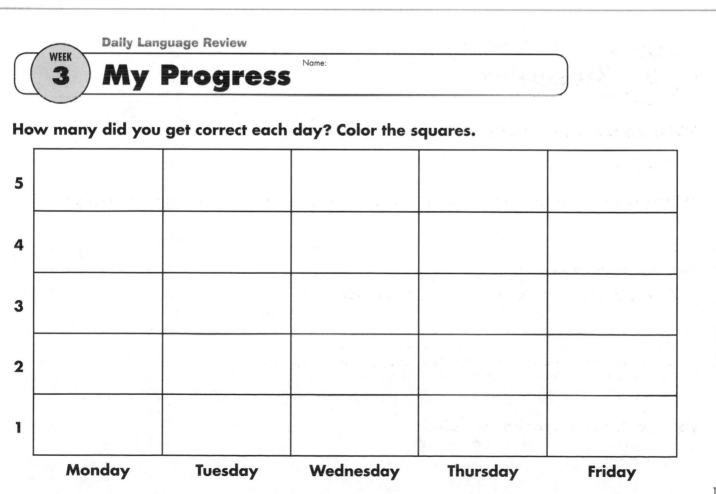

	Monday	Tuesday	Wednesday	Thursday	Friday
5					
4					
3					
2					
1					

WEEK 4

Monday

Name:

Correct these sentences.

1. on april 2 grandma avery will celebrate her hundred birthday

_____

2. i studied an interesting artical kayaking in alaska in world magazine

_____

Write the past tense of the verb *grow*.

3. _____

Write a fact about *Canada*.

4. _____

Circle the antonym for *pursue*.

5. chase   continue   abandon   study

WEEK 4

Tuesday

Name:

Choose the best word to complete this sentence.

1. She _____ have any coins in her pocket.
   don't   doesn't   never   always

Correct these sentences.

2. the old tyred dog wantz to lay down by the warm fire

_____

3. are we suppose to read the plains or the desert in are books

_____

Write the two words that make up this contraction.

4. you'd _____   _____

Use this homophone pair in one sentence: *forth, fourth*.

5. _____

© Evan-Moor Corp. • Daily Language Review • EMC 576

WEEK 4 Wednesday

Name: _____

Correct these sentences.

1. the scaryest story in *horrifying tales* was sounds by t s jones

_____

2. the farmer let 'em ride him horse

_____

Circle the adjectives in this sentence.

3. The graceful antelope leaped quickly over the rough, rocky roadbed and disappeared into the thick bushes beyond.

Write two words that rhyme with *thrown*.

4. _____   _____

Circle the word that is spelled correctly.

5. receive   receve   recieve   receeve

WEEK 4 Thursday

Name: _____

Circle the word that comes first in alphabetical order.

1. myth   mystery   myself   mysterious

Where is someone who is saying the following?

2. "Due to unexpected turbulence, the captain has turned on the Fasten Seatbelt sign."

_____

Correct these sentences.

3. dad sets in a chair to read him newspaper

_____

4. is miss browns english class gonna resight robert frosts poem

_____

Which part of speech is underlined: noun, verb, adjective, or adverb?

5. Lay the new clothes <u>neatly</u> on the bed before you go outside. _____

WEEK 4 **Friday**

Name: _____

© Evan-Moor Corp. • Daily Language Review • EMC 576

Combine the following sentences to make one sentence.

1. The dog chased the cat. The cat ran up the tree.

   _____

2. Seline needed to buy a new dress. Seline was performing in a concert.

   _____

3. Tom and Seth hit home runs. The team won the championship game.

   _____

4. Would you like some lemonade to drink? Would you like some cookies to eat?

   _____

5. I am very hungry. I think I could eat a horse.

   _____

WEEK 4 **My Progress**

Name: _____

© Evan-Moor Corp. • Daily Language Review • EMC 576

How many did you get correct each day? Color the squares.

	Monday	Tuesday	Wednesday	Thursday	Friday
5					
4					
3					
2					
1					

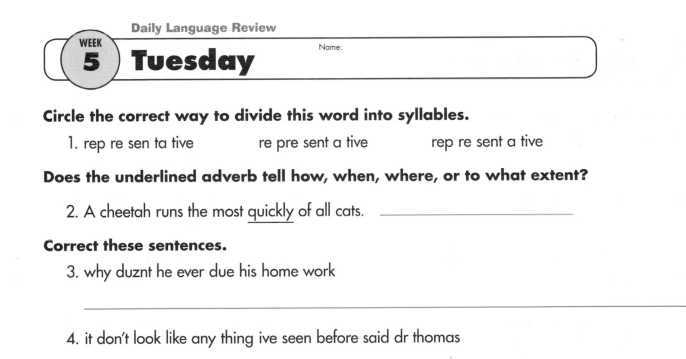

WEEK 5 Monday

Name: _____

Correct these sentences.

1. "carl will you help me do home work afterschool"

_____

2. "no not today because I'm going somewhere with my mom"

_____

Rewrite this phrase, using a possessive noun.

3. the video game belonging to Scott _____

Choose the best word to complete this sentence.

4. _____ going to meet us in the lobby after the movie.

    Their   There   They's   They're

What is the meaning of this figure of speech?

5. When I asked her for a loan, she said, "Go fly a kite."

_____

Daily Language Review

WEEK 5 Tuesday

Name: _____

Circle the correct way to divide this word into syllables.

1. rep re sen ta tive   re pre sent a tive   rep re sent a tive

Does the underlined adverb tell how, when, where, or to what extent?

2. A cheetah runs the most <u>quickly</u> of all cats. _____

Correct these sentences.

3. why duznt he ever due his home work

_____

4. it don't look like any thing ive seen before said dr thomas

_____

Circle the cause and underline the effects.

5. The lava oozed down the sides of the volcano, and black smoke smothered the sunlight after the eruption.

WEEK 5 **Wednesday**   Name:

Correct these sentences.

1. after im done skateing ill go to the liburary four a hour

_____

2. did you get a letter from youre pen pal

_____

Which part of speech is underlined: noun, verb, adjective, or adverb?

3. The <u>flickering</u> candles stood at attention in the frosting drifts. _____

Synonyms or antonyms?

4. reluctant, eager _____

Circle the correct abbreviation for *Michigan*.

5. MIC   MI   MN   MH

© Evan-Moor Corp. • Daily Language Review • EMC 576

WEEK 5 **Thursday**   Name:

Write the past and future tenses of the verb *drip*.

1. Past: _____   Future: _____

Rewrite this phrase, using a possessive noun.

2. the tusks and ears of the elephant _____

Correct these sentences.

3. we stoped to use the bathroom stretch and eat diner

_____

4. two boys bikes was left in the senter of fivth street on friday aprl 1

_____

Declarative, interrogative, imperative, or exclamatory?

5. I went to the soccer game with Leon last Saturday. _____

© Evan-Moor Corp. • Daily Language Review • EMC 576

WEEK 5 Friday

Name:

Circle the best word to complete each analogy.

1. *Cub* is to *lion* as *foal* is to _____.

       colt   dog   zebra   monkey

2. *Hat* is to *head* as *lid* is to _____.

       jar   cover   hair   beret

3. *Picture* is to *frame* as *cream* is to _____.

      butter   cup   pitcher   whipped

4. *Dog* is to *leash* as *balloon* is to _____.

      cloud   branch   helium   string

5. *Tennis* is to *racket* as *volleyball* is to _____.

      net   hand   basket   court

WEEK 5 My Progress

Name:

How many did you get correct each day? Color the squares.

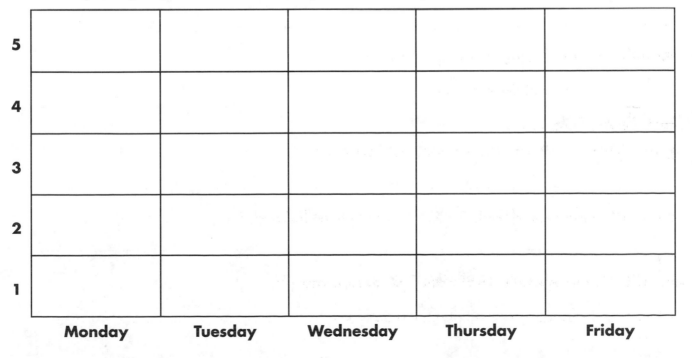

	Monday	Tuesday	Wednesday	Thursday	Friday
5					
4					
3					
2					
1					

WEEK 6 Monday

Name: _____

Correct these sentences.

1. mrs lee have traveled to europ asia and south america

_____

2. i cant weight to travel by myself

_____

Use context clues to determine the meaning of the bolded word.

3. Climbing to the rock ledge will test his skills and his **mettle**.

_____

Write two synonyms for *mistaken*.

4. _____   _____

Fiction or nonfiction?

5. Unopened flower buds of the clove tree are used to dull
   the pain of a toothache, freshen breath, and flavor ham. _____

WEEK 6 Tuesday

Name: _____

Does the underlined adjective tell which one, what kind, or how many?

1. Carlos exclaimed, "Look at that <u>huge</u> pumpkin!" _____

Circle the predicate in this sentence.

2. The whiskers on my kitten twitch when I rub its back.

Correct these sentences.

3. derek sad he was two busy too make his bed

_____

4. bob lee and al went to the steinhart aquarium to see the shark

_____

Circle the word that is not spelled correctly.

5. inconsiderate   uncomfortable   prejudice   preveiw

© Evan-Moor Corp. • Daily Language Review • EMC 576

WEEK 6

Wednesday

Name:

Correct these sentences.

1. every saterday myh brother watches *iron chef*

_____

2. last sumer my friend tara moved to taos new mexico

_____

Choose the best word to complete this analogy.

3. seldom : many :: often : _____

   lots   more   few   several

Synonyms, antonyms, or homophones?

4. quick, speedy _____

5. week, weak _____

WEEK 6

Thursday

Name:

Write the contraction that is made from these two words.

1. we are _____

Rewrite this word, adding a prefix.

2. test _____

Correct these sentences.

3. if we work hard replied judy well earn a good grade

_____

4. michael ask how soon will brakefast be ready

_____

Past, present, or future?

5. occupied _____

WEEK 6 **Friday**

Name:

Circle the correct word to complete each sentence.

1. How _____ did you do on the test?   good   well

2. _____ puppies are growing bigger every day.   Are   Our

3. _____ that woman standing by the car?   Who's   Whose

4. Do you know _____ jacket that is?   who's   whose

5. When _____ the book reports due?   are   our

© Evan-Moor Corp. • Daily Language Review • EMC 576

WEEK 6 **My Progress**

Name:

How many did you get correct each day? Color the squares.

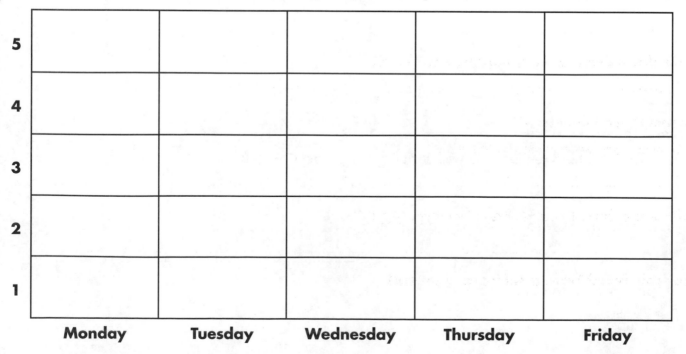

	Monday	Tuesday	Wednesday	Thursday	Friday
5					
4					
3					
2					
1					

© Evan-Moor Corp. • Daily Language Review • EMC 576

WEEK 7 **Monday**

Name: _____

Correct these sentences.

1. that john elway football belongs to my brother and I

   _____

2. michael and me ran in the big brothers marathon

   _____

Use these three homophones in one sentence: *there, their, they're.*

3. _____

   _____

Circle the preposition in this sentence.

4. A young boy is hurrying along the crowded sidewalk.

Write a word that would belong in this group.

5. speak   utter   verbalize   inform   _____

WEEK 7 **Tuesday**

Name: _____

Write an antonym for this word.

1. ancient _____

Circle the word that is not spelled correctly.

2. wrestle   whistel   knapsack   scratch

Correct these sentences.

3. every one were invited to there party

   _____

4. several butterflys and eagels flew over head

   _____

Does this word have a suffix or a prefix?

5. impolite _____

WEEK 7 · Wednesday

Name:

Correct these sentences.

1. them womens lunchs all cost the same amoount

_____

2. jim likes apple cherry and peach pie but I only like cake

_____

Write the root or base word.

3. prehistoric _____

Simile or metaphor?

4. When the principal walked by, Sam sat as still as a statue. _____

Is _after_ used as a preposition or an adverb in this sentence?

5. After the farmer harvested the corn, he sold it as ensilage. _____

WEEK 7 · Thursday

Name:

Write the number of syllables in each word.

1. inconvenient _____

2. inconsiderate _____

Correct these sentences.

3. mi sister teared off the books cover

_____

4. park city hired a couch for the boys sports teams

_____

Write the pronoun that would replace the underlined words.

5. The soldiers and their prisoners marched in single file. _____

WEEK 7 — Friday

Name:

EMC 576

Match the words with the correct definitions.

1. intersection   a. the rate at which something happens

2. vertical   b. a mathematical statement

3. equation   c. straight up and down

4. currency   d. a place where one thing crosses another

5. frequency   e. the money used in a country

WEEK 7 — My Progress

Name:

How many did you get correct each day? Color the squares.

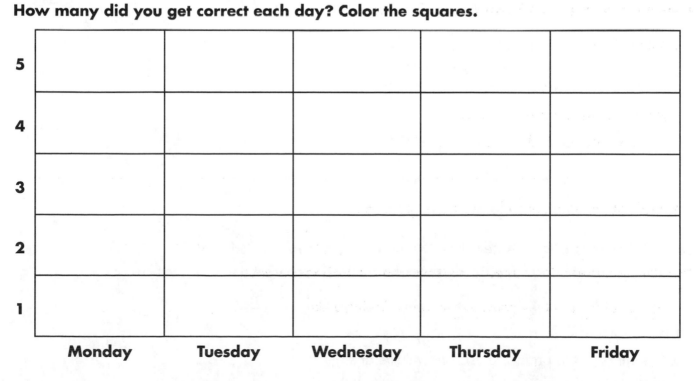

	Monday	Tuesday	Wednesday	Thursday	Friday
5					
4					
3					
2					
1					

WEEK 8 **Monday**

Name: _____

© Evan-Moor Corp. • Daily Language Review • EMC 576

Correct these sentences.

1. please tell me the answer to the riddel begged jose

_____

2. will you help them guys paint there fence

_____

Is the comma used correctly? Circle *yes* or *no*.

3. August 31, 2009   Yes   No

4. Salina Kansas, 76532   Yes   No

Which part of speech is underlined: noun, verb, adjective, or adverb?

5. We offer the largest <u>selection</u> of cool beverages, tasty meals, and luscious desserts in town.

_____

WEEK 8 **Tuesday**

Name: _____

© Evan-Moor Corp. • Daily Language Review • EMC 576

Choose the best word to complete this analogy.

1. leaf : spinach :: root : _____
   flower   carrot   tomato   lettuce

Correct these sentences.

2. jeff sits his glasses on the tabel

_____

3. I need to right a thank you note for the gift my aunt sent me

_____

Use the context clues to determine the meaning of the bolded word.

4. The party next door was a big **distraction** as I tried to concentrate on my homework.

_____

Fact or opinion?

5. It is important to protect forests and wildlife at any cost. _____

WEEK 8 Wednesday

Name:

Correct these sentences.

1. we read articles form newsweek time and cricket

_____

2. while she pourd tea the girl spilt it on he mothers desk

_____

Circle the word that comes first in alphabetical order.

3. feminine   fellowship   femoral   feline

Circle the word that is spelled correctly.

4. neithur   worrys   gratious   siege

Circle the adjectives in this sentence.

5. The fierce winds surged across the carefully planted wheat fields.

WEEK 8 Thursday

Name:

Name this part of a friendly letter.

1. Your friend, _____

What do the words in this group have in common?

2. biology   chemistry   anatomy   nuclear physics

_____

Correct these sentences.

3. whil I weighted for the griddel to git hot I drawded a desighn

_____

4. the sky opened up and rein slamed to the grownd

_____

Write the contraction that is made from these two words.

5. must not _____

© Evan-Moor Corp. • Daily Language Review • EMC 576

WEEK 8

Friday

Name:

Read the following paragraph and decide if the underlined parts have a capitalization error, a punctuation error, a spelling error, or no error.

The kendo competition was about to begin at the Obon Festival. In traditional dress, the
‾‾‾‾‾‾‾‾‾‾‾‾‾‾‾‾‾‾‾‾‾‾
  1   **2**

competitors moved like frajle dancers around the ring. Briefly lunging toward each other and
                       ‾‾‾‾‾‾‾‾‾‾‾‾‾‾‾‾‾‾‾‾‾‾‾‾‾ ‾‾‾
                                  3   **4**

then stepping back the competitors performed. Watch the graceful warriors fencing.
‾‾‾‾‾‾‾‾‾‾‾‾‾‾‾‾‾‾‾‾   ‾‾‾‾‾‾‾‾‾‾‾‾‾‾‾‾‾‾‾‾‾‾‾‾‾‾‾‾‾‾‾‾‾‾‾‾
                                                              5

1. _____

2. _____

3. _____

4. _____

5. _____

© Evan-Moor Corp. • Daily Language Review • EMC 576

WEEK 8

My Progress

Name:

How many did you get correct each day? Color the squares.

	Monday	Tuesday	Wednesday	Thursday	Friday
5					
4					
3					
2					
1					

© Evan-Moor Corp. • Daily Language Review • EMC 576

WEEK 9 — Monday

Name: _____

Correct these sentences.

1. whose that there boy over their

_____

2. after the hen lies her eggs she sets on them

_____

Write a word that would belong in this group.

3. lakes   rivers   oceans   ponds   _____

What is personified in the following sentence?

4. The books on my shelf whispered secrets as I tried to go to sleep.

_____

Circle the word that is not spelled correctly.

5. orchestra   ordinery   dictionary   stare

WEEK 9 — Tuesday

Name: _____

Rewrlte this sentence, adding at least one adjective.

1. The puppy wagged its tail.

_____

What is the correct way to divide these words into syllables?

2. obstinate _____

3. occupant _____

Correct these sentences.

4. me and pete got a new dog at adams pet shop

_____

5. tim's shews are two big sew he will by a knew pare at ace shoestore

WEEK 9

Wednesday

Name: _____

Correct these sentences.

1. the new deskes in the class room belong to ana todd and kate

_____

2. uncle fred bot us pizza at freddies

_____

Is the bolded word a subject pronoun or an object pronoun?

3. The teacher trusted **him** to take attendance. _____

Choose the best word to complete this analogy.

4. *Predator* is to *prey* as *owl* is to _____.

   fly   mouse   hawk   talons

Combine these two ideas into a single sentence.

5. Susan got out of bed. She looked out her window to check the weather.

_____

WEEK 9

Thursday

Name: _____

Circle the correct abbreviation for *Road*.

1. R.   Rd.   RD.   Rd

Rewrite each word, using the suffix *-ing*.

2. receive _____ worry _____ plan _____

Correct these sentences.

3. constantly tom worrys about his end of the year projeckt

_____

4. the thersty boy drank the dr pepper in one swallough

_____

Synonyms or antonyms?

5. irregular, rough _____

WEEK 9 Friday

Name:

Read the paragraph. Underline the topic sentence and write the main idea. Then list three supporting details under the main idea.

Some seeds move on the wind. They have winglike parts to catch the wind. Other seeds have hooks or stickers. They catch in the fur of animals and are carried to new places. Some seeds float on water to new places. People move seeds, too. They plant them in their yards and gardens. Seeds travel in many different ways.

Main Idea: _____

_____

Details: 1. _____

2. _____

3. _____

WEEK 9 My Progress

Name:

How many did you get correct each day? Color the squares.

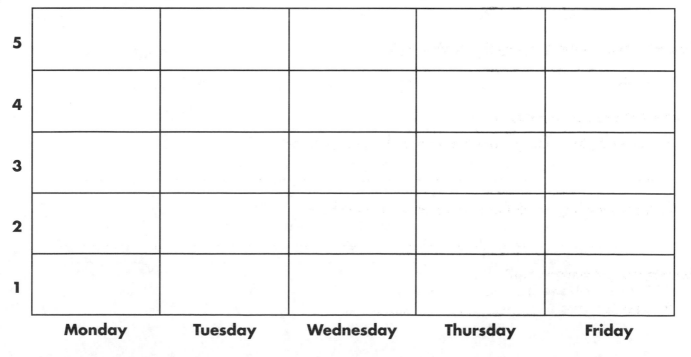

	Monday	Tuesday	Wednesday	Thursday	Friday
5					
4					
3					
2					
1					

WEEK 10 Monday

Name:

Correct these sentences.

1. native americans beleived that spirits protected them

_____

2. there was hundreds of tribes in america when christopher columbus landed

_____

Fact or fantasy?

3. People and animals can sink in quicksand. _____

Choose the best word to complete each sentence.

4. The trumpet's range is _____ than the baritone's.
   higher   highest   high   none of these

5. The tuba's range is _____ of all.
   lower   lowest   low   none of these

WEEK 10 Tuesday

Name:

Write an opinion about *pollution*.

1. _____

If the guide words on a dictionary page are *penicillin* and *pepper*, which word would not be on the page?

2. peninsula   peony   penniless   peppermint   people

Correct these sentences.

3. i have the adresses of frends living in other countrys

_____

4. mrs moores busnesses is taking pitchers of familee groups

_____

Use this homophone pair in one sentence: *for, four*.

5. _____

WEEK 10 Wednesday

Name:

Correct these sentences.

1. the climit along the equator is diffrent from the climit in alaska

_____

2. his vehicul had a puntured tire and sew he waited by the syde of the rode

_____

Write the present tense of the verb _caught_.

3. _____

Declarative, interrogative, imperative, or exclamatory?

4. Watch out for the hole in the deck. _____

Underline the subject in this sentence.

5. How many purchases were made on Sunday?

WEEK 10 Thursday

Name:

Circle the word that comes last in alphabetical order.

1. shudder   shuffle   shut   shutdown   shuttle

Write the plural of each noun.

2. fox _____   wolf _____

Correct these sentences.

3. mr tuttle asked did you studee four you're math test

_____

4. I spended a day at the libary writing my essae for english

_____

Write the complete predicate of this sentence.

5. Our friendship has lasted a long time, despite our differences.

_____

WEEK 10 Friday

Name: _____

© Evan-Moor Corp. • Daily Language Review • EMC 576

What do the underlined phrases mean?

1. Mrs. Peters said that the new easel would <u>fill the bill.</u>

   _____

2. My grandpa is nearly ninety, but he's <u>fit as a fiddle.</u>

   _____

3. The custodian said that she'd <u>get to the bottom</u> of the graffiti on the wall.

   _____

4. Lance has <u>his finger in every pie.</u>

   _____

5. Your dad will never double your allowance. <u>Get real!</u>

   _____

WEEK 10 My Progress

Name: _____

© Evan-Moor Corp. • Daily Language Review • EMC 576

How many did you get correct each day? Color the squares.

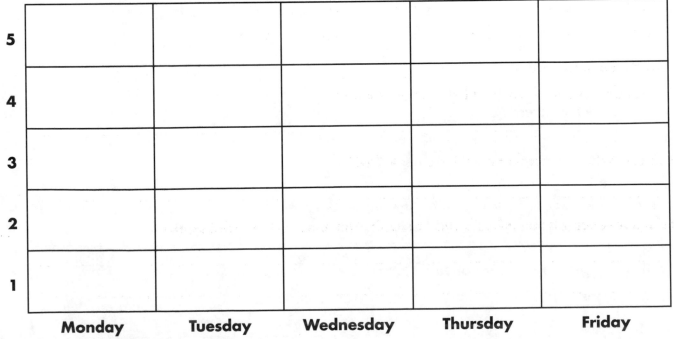

	Monday	Tuesday	Wednesday	Thursday	Friday
5					
4					
3					
2					
1					

WEEK 11 Monday

Name:

Correct these sentences.

1. the words impolight and inkonsiderate are close in meaning

_____

2. dr landrys motto is always bee prepeared

_____

Rewrite this word, using a suffix.

3. strange _____

Simile or metaphor?

4. Her hair was as shiny as a blackbird's wing. _____

Write a word that would belong in this group.

5. calm   soothe   still   allay   _____

WEEK 11 Tuesday

Name:

Circle the words in each row that rhyme.

1. cruel   school   tell   cool   rule   role
2. chute   newt   shut   route   suit   stool

Correct these sentences.

3. "well dew you think you can help me on saterday"

_____

4. "i can help you monday jay if thats not to layt"

_____

Write a sentence about *wheels* that contains an example of alliteration.

5. _____

_____

WEEK 11 Wednesday

Name: _____

Correct these sentences.

1. all the ice in the lemonaide begun to disapear

_____

2. the jelly in slim's sandwitch driped out onto hiz shirt

_____

Circle the words that have four syllables.

3. representative   technology   currency   substituted

Circle the cause and underline the effect.

4. The ticket line was so long that we missed the first part of the movie.

Write a common noun for each proper noun.

5. Mr. Beckman _____   Arlington, Virginia _____

© Evan-Moor Corp. • Daily Language Review • EMC 576

WEEK 11 Thursday

Name: _____

Write the comparative and superlative adjectives for *heavy*.

1. Comparative: _____   Superlative: _____

Synonyms, antonyms, or homophones?

2. substitute, switch _____

Correct these sentences.

3. we catch that there bus at the corner of elm street and first avenue

_____

4. traveler airlines allows you to take one suit case and a carry on bag

_____

Choose the best word to complete this sentence.

5. The _____ of his aftershave lingered in the room.

     cent   scent   sent

© Evan-Moor Corp. • Daily Language Review • EMC 576

WEEK 11 Friday

Name:

Write each of these suffixes next to its meaning below.

ly   less   ar   ful   ment   or

1. full of   _____

2. the condition of   _____

3. without   _____

4. in what manner   _____

5. one who   _____

WEEK 11 My Progress

Name:

How many did you get correct each day? Color the squares.

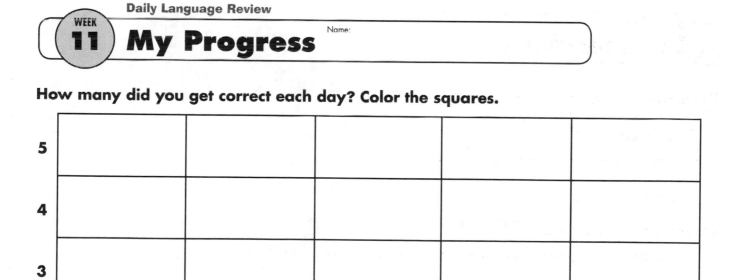

	Monday	Tuesday	Wednesday	Thursday	Friday
5					
4					
3					
2					
1					

WEEK 12 Monday

Name: _____

© Evan-Moor Corp. • Daily Language Review • EMC 576

Correct these sentences.

1. the paddel boats moved along the missouri river

_____

2. land ahoy the first mate shouted

_____

Use the context clues to determine the meaning of the bolded word.

3. Although he'd never signed an agreement, his **tacit** understanding of the law was clear.

_____

Circle the word that is spelled correctly.

4. amphibean   enviroment   performance   temperature   campain

Circle the adjectives in this sentence.

5. The heavily armored crocodile slid slowly from the mossy banks into the dark depths.

WEEK 12 Tuesday

Name: _____

© Evan-Moor Corp. • Daily Language Review • EMC 576

What part of speech is underlined?

1. Can an amphibian live <u>in an environment</u> where the temperature is very low?

_____

Correct these sentences.

2. we wont have an asignment untill wedesday september 3

_____

3. they're were three peaces of pizza on the plait kelly took the larger one

_____

Circle the prepositions in this sentence.

4. I went to the soccer game with my friend Leon.

Write a synonym for this word.

5. stalk _____

38

WEEK 12 Wednesday

Name:

Correct these sentences.

1. six geeses was searching for sum delishush worms to eat

_____

2. last year we spended our vacashion at uncle jims farm

_____

Choose the best words to complete this analogy.

3. jack : flat tire :: hammer : _____
   dull pencil   broken window   deflated ball   loose board

Choose the best word to complete this sentence.

4. _____ your closest living relative?
   Whose   Who's   Who

Circle the adverb in this sentence.

5. Several flew overhead.

WEEK 12 Thursday

Name:

Fact or opinion?

1. Water expands when it is frozen. _____

Are the underlined words a common noun or a proper noun?

2. The students swarmed across the playground and splashed into the <u>community pool</u>.

_____

Correct these sentences.

3. The hail stones pounded the roofs during the storem

_____

4. dr rivers standed besighed his pateinces bed and said say ahhhh

_____

Write an antonym for _rude_.

5. _____

WEEK 12 Friday

Name:

**Read the words in each line and mark *sentence* or *not a sentence*.
In each line, circle the subject and underline the predicate.**

1. Climbed the mountain and camped   ◯ sentence   ◯ not a sentence

2. The machine responded to his command   ◯ sentence   ◯ not a sentence

3. Always in motion and chattering too, the young toddler   ◯ sentence   ◯ not a sentence

4. Tom, Franco, Seline, and Julie played   ◯ sentence   ◯ not a sentence

5. He lurched and stumbled against the table   ◯ sentence   ◯ not a sentence

---

WEEK 12 My Progress

Name:

How many did you get correct each day? Color the squares.

5					
4					
3					
2					
1					
	Monday	**Tuesday**	**Wednesday**	**Thursday**	**Friday**

WEEK 13 Monday — Name:

Correct these sentences.

1. werent their no cookies left

_____

2. hello out there terrys voice was muffled by his mask

_____

Circle the preposition in this sentence.

3. Two delivery trucks pulled into the parking lot.

Choose the best word to complete this sentence.

4. Do you know the recipe very _____?
   easy   good   well   none of these

Divide this word into syllables.

5. standardize _____

WEEK 13 Tuesday — Name:

Choose the best word to complete this analogy.

1. *Shallow* is to *deep* as *imaginary* is to _____.
   make-believe   fiction   authentic   hard-headed

Are the underlined words the subject or the predicate?

2. The outcome of the game depends on us. _____

Correct these sentences.

3. why cant he never git here on thyme

_____

4. the singers will end the show with there version of its a small worlde

_____

Fact or opinion?

5. Honey is a nutritious natural food. _____

WEEK
13 **Wednesday**   Name:

© Evan-Moor Corp. • Daily Language Review • EMC 576

Correct these sentences.

1. the sioux lived on the great plains and trackt bufalo

_____

2. woodland tribes like the onondaga maid they're homes of wood

_____

Complete this analogy.

3. *cm* is to *centimeter* as *yd* is to _____.

Circle the word that is not spelled correctly.

4. distruction   division   infection   attention   description

Write a pronoun that would replace the underlined noun.

5. The <u>custodians</u> worked hard to get ready for the open house. _____

WEEK
13 **Thursday**   Name:

© Evan-Moor Corp. • Daily Language Review • EMC 576

Write the contraction that is made from these two words.

1. they are   _____

What print reference source would you use to find out about the world's largest volcanoes?

2. _____

Correct these sentences.

3. whos going to kollect the six oclock male when its delivred

_____

4. ive know idea what your talking about

_____

Write a synonym for *cruel*.

5. _____

WEEK 13 Friday

Name:

© Evan-Moor Corp. • Daily Language Review • EMC 576

Read the following paragraph and decide if the underlined parts have a capitalization error, a punctuation error, a spelling error, or no error.

The first olympic games were held in Olympus Greece, in 776 B.C. Todays Olympic
<u>   1   </u>   <u>2</u>   <u>3</u>

competitions include many different sports. Approximatly 10,500 athletes participated in the
                                                      <u>4</u>

2008 Summer Games in Beijing.
          <u>5</u>

1. _____

2. _____

3. _____

4. _____

5. _____

WEEK 13 My Progress

Name:

How many did you get correct each day? Color the squares.

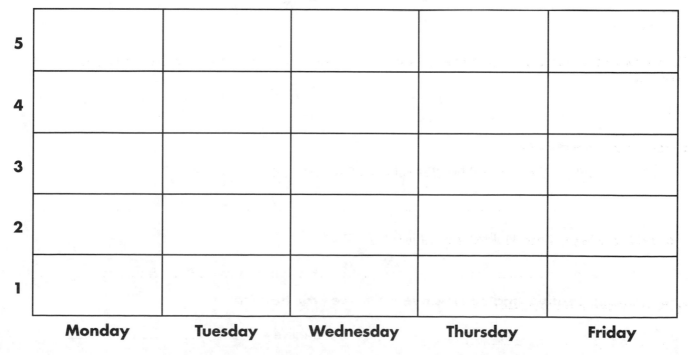

	Monday	Tuesday	Wednesday	Thursday	Friday
5					
4					
3					
2					
1					

© Evan-Moor Corp. • Daily Language Review • EMC 576

WEEK 14 Monday

Name:

© Evan-Moor Corp. • Daily Language Review • EMC 576

Correct these sentences.

1. my most faverit candys are miad out of swiss chocalate

_____

2. borises baby sister torn the libray book pages

_____

Write the base or root word.

3. condensation _____

What is the meaning of this figure of speech?

4. That game <u>is for the birds.</u> I wish we could get a new one.

_____

Write the complete subject of this sentence.

5. The stunt diver used an oxygen tank until he reached the surface.

_____

WEEK 14 Tuesday

Name:

© Evan-Moor Corp. • Daily Language Review • EMC 576

Write the plural form of this noun.

1. radius _____

Choose the best words to complete this sentence.

2. When I go to _____ aquarium, I always take _____ guidebook to help me identify the fish.
             a   an   a   an

Correct these sentences.

3. the dogs owners writed a pome about they're pet

_____

4. can you play quiet untill the meeting is adjurned

_____

Write the comparative and superlative adjectives for *handsome*.

5. Comparative: _____ Superlative: _____

WEEK 14 Wednesday Name:

Correct these sentences.

1. h w longfellow wrote listen my children and you shall here of the mid-night ride of paul revere

_____

2. the wether caster toled the temperture explaned the fog and gave a forecaste

_____

Use context clues to determine the meaning of the bolded words.

3. The volunteers were always willing to **step into the breach** and offer assistance to the tornado victims.

_____

Write the past tense of these verbs.

4. bind   _____

5. weep   _____

WEEK 14 Thursday Name:

Is the bolded letter a subject pronoun or an object pronoun?

1. The teacher and **I** presented the awards at the assembly.   _____

What part of speech is underlined in this sentence?

2. Green grasshoppers <u>gracefully</u> glide in gravity-defying leaps.   _____

Correct these sentences.

3. I will lie the photograf on that table in plane view

_____

4. flowers of every color bloomd in professer shaws garden

_____

What is the meaning of this figure of speech?

5. I'll tell you where Mom keeps the cookies, but you've got to <u>keep it under your hat.</u>

_____

WEEK 14 Friday

Name:

© Evan-Moor Corp. • Daily Language Review • EMC 576

Combine the sentences to make one sentence.

1. The football team ran onto the field. They carried their helmets in their hands.

   _____

2. Pam found a book for her report. She used the library browser on the computer. Pam checked out the book.

   _____

3. Tom fell off the bike. He learned that racing bikes can be dangerous.

   _____

4. Ahmad is our new student body president. He got the most votes in the election.

   _____

5. Ashley lives next door to me. She feeds my puppies when I'm gone.

   _____

WEEK 14 My Progress

Name:

© Evan-Moor Corp. • Daily Language Review • EMC 576

How many did you get correct each day? Color the squares.

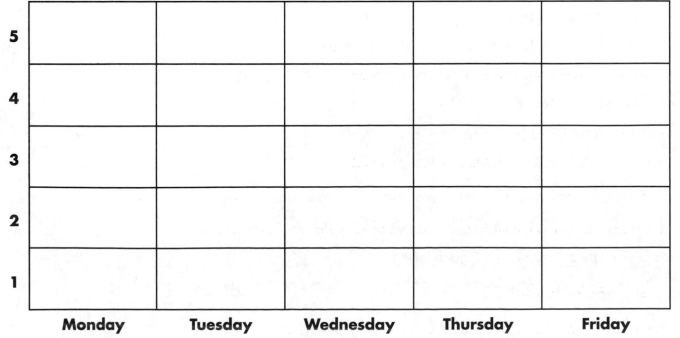

	Monday	Tuesday	Wednesday	Thursday	Friday
5					
4					
3					
2					
1					

WEEK 15 Monday

Name: _____

Correct these sentences.

1. due you think mr long will except my report if its hand written

_____

2. my grandad believes you shuld always carry a hankercheif

_____

Circle the preposition in this sentence.

3. Students use spoken and written language for many different purposes.

Simile or metaphor?

4. I wandered across the meadow, a lonely cloud in a clear blue sky. _____

Circle the words that are not spelled correctly.

5. several   numerel   vowal   hundred   toward

WEEK 15 Tuesday

Name: _____

Choose the best word to complete this analogy.

1. down : pillow :: beans : _____
   beanstalk   beanie   bed   beanbag

Circle the correct abbreviation for *Boulevard*.

2. Bvd.   blvd   Blvd.   bd

Correct these sentences.

3. if I was a docter I wood help people stay well

_____

4. county hospital is located on the corner of king way and state street

_____

Past, present, or future?

5. wander _____

© Evan-Moor Corp. • Daily Language Review • EMC 576

WEEK 15 Wednesday

© Evan-Moor Corp. • Daily Language Review • EMC 576

Name:

Correct these sentences.

1. my brothers bestest riddle is what kind of house ways the least

_____

2. the anser is a lite house

_____

What do the words in this group have in common?

3. rectangle   trapezoid   square   triangle   parallelogram

_____

If the guide words on a dictionary page are _hungry_ and _hyacinth_, which words would not be on the page?

4. hurl   hydrangea   hustle   hunger   hutch

Does the underlined adverb tell how, when, where, or to what extent?

5. Tommy quickly ran <u>behind</u> the house. _____

WEEK 15 Thursday

© Evan-Moor Corp. • Daily Language Review • EMC 576

Name:

Does this word have a prefix or a suffix?

1. misunderstand _____

Write the singular form of this noun.

2. halves _____

Correct these sentences.

3. mrs turlock says that I must learn how to use parenthesis

_____

4. I cant imagin a more ridiculus idea

_____

Synonyms or antonyms?

5. free, restricted _____

WEEK 15 Friday

Name:

Identify the subject and verb or verbs in each sentence.

1. She crept past the baby's crib.

   Subject: _____ Verb(s): _____

2. She loved to walk in the rain.

   Subject: _____ Verb(s): _____

3. Toby gave his mother the report.

   Subject: _____ Verb(s): _____

4. Tomorrow I'd like to leave early.

   Subject: _____ Verb(s): _____

5. The three girls smiled and clapped their hands.

   Subject: _____ Verb(s): _____

WEEK 15 My Progress

Name:

How many did you get correct each day? Color the squares.

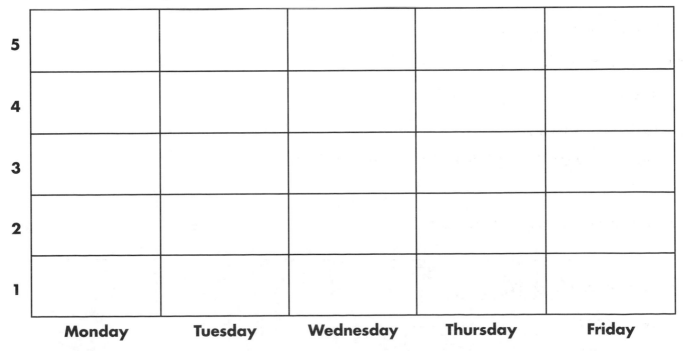

	Monday	Tuesday	Wednesday	Thursday	Friday
5					
4					
3					
2					
1					

Monday
Name:

Correct these sentences.

1. scott make your arms slice into the water shouted couch storm

_____

2. he reminded him keep your kick going strong out of you're turns

_____

Circle the cause and underline the effect.

3. I didn't understand the questions on the test because I missed the previous class.

Add the correct punctuation to this business greeting.

4. To Whom It May Concern

Use this homophone pair in one sentence: _billed, build_.

5. _____

Tuesday
Name:

If the guide words on a dictionary page are _feedback_ and _fencing_, which words would be on the page?

1. feel   feeble   felon   fence   fender

Correct these sentences.

2. I all ready finishd doing the dishus mom sighed

_____

3. please she said put your dirtee plait on the drain bored before you leaf

_____

Write the root or base word.

4. effective _____

Write the plural form of this noun.

5. sandbox _____

WEEK 16 Wednesday   Name:

Correct these sentences.

1. the waitriss said to day we have strawberrys raspberrys and blackberrys

_____

2. wood you like some whipt cream with you're berrys she asked

_____

Declarative, interrogative, imperative, or exclamatory?

3. Look out below! _____

Is the bolded word a subject pronoun or an object pronoun?

4. Hot or cold, **they** tasted great! _____

Circle the words that have three syllables.

5. entrance   entertain   envision   enviable   envelope

WEEK 16 Thursday   Name:

What print reference source would you use to find the boundary between Egypt and Israel?

1. _____

Real or make-believe?

2. The cheetahs ran free in the Kenyan game park while tourists watched from their jeeps.

_____

Correct these sentences.

3. the baby looked like shes going to ball

_____

4. the baby sitter ask do you have any ideas about what we shud do

_____

What part of speech is underlined?

5. The cheering crowd <u>roared</u> as the ball cleared the fence. _____

WEEK 16 Friday

Name: _____

Write the verb forms for each verb.

	Present	Past	Past Participle (used with *has*, *had*, or *have*)
1. am	_____	_____	_____
2. come	_____	_____	_____
3. do	_____	_____	_____
4. eat	_____	_____	_____
5. see	_____	_____	_____

WEEK 16 My Progress

Name: _____

How many did you get correct each day? Color the squares.

	Monday	Tuesday	Wednesday	Thursday	Friday
5					
4					
3					
2					
1					

WEEK 17 Monday

Name:

Correct these sentences.

1. at midnight wee heared jims frends searching for snacs in the cuboard

_____

2. how meny cartens comed in the maail shipmant this after noon

_____

Are the underlined words part of the subject or part of the predicate?

3. Lay the baby in her crib <u>so she can take a nap.</u> _____

Add punctuation to this address.

4. 5430 Broad Ave #310

Oakland CA 94618

Write an opinion about _endangered species._

5. _____

WEEK 17 Tuesday

Name:

Write the two words that make up this contraction.

1. there've _____   _____

Synonyms or antonyms?

2. surpass, exceed _____

Correct these sentences.

3. who's dog are them over their

_____

4. I wish I cud stay at home too meat you but I have two go

_____

Underline the prepositional phrase in this sentence.

5. Carla's friend Margo came for a long visit.

WEEK 17

Wednesday

Name:

Correct these sentences.

1. nurse nancy gived her a cleen bandadge four her kne

_____

2. it may not seem write but its all ways been the rule

_____

Complete this analogy.

3. *Minute* is to *clock* as *ounce* is to _____.

Choose the best word to complete this sentence.

4. Yesterday he _____ his hat on the peg by the door.

   hang   hanged   hung   will hang   has hung

Use this homophone pair in one sentence: *wood, would*.

5. _____

WEEK 17

Thursday

Name:

Circle the word that is not spelled correctly.

1. multiply   currency   vertical   manufacture   atmophere

Proper noun or common noun?

2. the priest   _____

3. Father McGovern   _____

Correct these sentences.

4. i cant weight to try the snacks nicole made cake sara made candy and bob made pie

_____

5. farmer ted dug a whole in hiz garten for a compost pit

_____

Write the plural of each noun. Then write how you made the word plural.

1. president _____

_____

2. bench _____

_____

3. variety _____

_____

4. journey _____

_____

5. life _____

_____

© Evan-Moor Corp. • Daily Language Review • EMC 576

How many did you get correct each day? Color the squares.

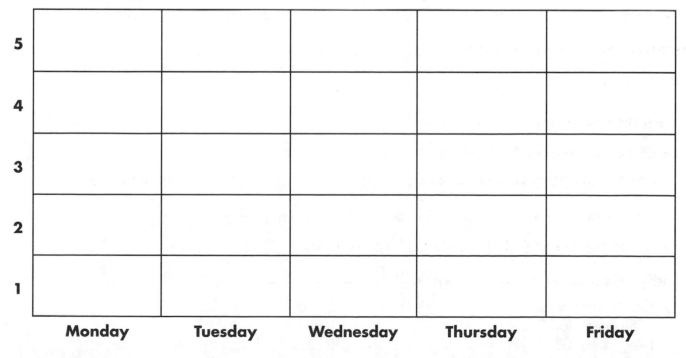

	Monday	Tuesday	Wednesday	Thursday	Friday
5					
4					
3					
2					
1					

© Evan-Moor Corp. • Daily Language Review • EMC 576

WEEK 18 Monday

Name: _____

Correct these sentences.

1. sasha whispered to her self where did john hid moms ring

_____

2. i read to chapters of *tom sawyer* every knight before I go two bed

_____

Use context clues to determine the meaning of the bolded word.

3. My older sister is always running into things because she is **oblivious** to her surroundings.

_____

Choose from these words to complete the sentence: *ware, wear, where.*

4. _____ can Teresa find a costume to _____ to the party?

If the guide words on a dictionary page are *ringing* and *ripple,* which word would be on the page?

5. ringed   rind   rinsing   rise   riptide

WEEK 18 Tuesday

Name: _____

Write the correct contraction for *of the clock.*

1. _____

Use this homophone pair in one sentence: *attendance, attendants.*

2. _____

Correct these sentences.

3. the dishs on the shelfs fell during the earth quake

_____

4. the mountian in the paynting is mtt hood said the museum giude

_____

Identify this part of a business letter.

5. The Western Stage
   165 Homestead Street
   Tyler, Texas 03673   _____

© Evan-Moor Corp. • Daily Language Review • EMC 576

WEEK 18 Wednesday

Name:

© Evan-Moor Corp. • Daily Language Review • EMC 576

Correct these sentences.

1. mrs springs drys floweres for bouguets

_____

2. the park acrosst the street from mi house is called central park

_____

Is the bolded word a subject pronoun or an object pronoun?

3. Did you see **her** wave her hand?   _____

Fact or opinion?

4. Mayan architects were some of the world's best builders.   _____

Do the underlined adjectives tell which one, what kind, or how many?

5. Lacy curtains were draped across the clear glass of the windows.

_____

WEEK 18 Thursday

Name:

© Evan-Moor Corp. • Daily Language Review • EMC 576

Is the underlined word a common noun or a proper noun?

1. The captain readied the plane for takeoff.   _____

Declarative, interrogative, imperative, or exclamatory?

2. Before a big test, is it more important to sleep or study?   _____

Correct these sentences.

3. aunt jo had to fly to denver on her weigh to st louis

_____

4. put extra rightin paper scissor pencils and glue in the tub

_____

Synonyms, antonyms, or homophones?

5. affirm, deny   _____

WEEK 18 — Friday

Name: _____

Read the following paragraph and decide if the underlined parts have a capitalization error, a punctuation error, a spelling error, or no error.

The spoted salamander remains almost unchanged from the first salamander that walked on The
    1   **2**   **3**

Earth about 330 Million years ago. It lives in caves, under rocks, and logs, and moves only
                      4   **5**

during the blackest hours of the night.

1. _____

2. _____

3. _____

4. _____

5. _____

WEEK 18 — My Progress

Name: _____

How many did you get correct each day? Color the squares.

	Monday	Tuesday	Wednesday	Thursday	Friday
5					
4					
3					
2					
1					

WEEK 19 Monday

Name: _____

Correct these sentences.

1. noone in the familee had ever bin to hawaii

_____

2. how meny boxs of cookys did you sell the troop leader ask

_____

Does the underlined adverb tell how, when, where, or to what extent?

3. The man danced <u>gracefully</u> across the floor. _____

Choose the best word to complete this sentence.

4. The hen named Peanut laid _____ eggs last month than the one named Annie.

       few   less   fewer   lesser

Circle the correct way to divide this word into syllables.

5. lia bil i ty   li abil i ty   li a bil i ty   li a bil it y

---

WEEK 19 Tuesday

Name: _____

Choose the best word to complete this analogy.

1. *Opaque* is to *transparent* as *turmoil* is to _____.

    peaceful   turbulent   stormy   clear

Circle the word that does not belong in this group.

2. oak   maple   pine   geranium   elm

Correct these sentences.

3. to me new years day means grandmas chili and a family feast

_____

4. the principle said make sure your children has a quite time for home work

_____

Declarative, interrogative, imperative, or exclamatory?

5. The shark in the aquarium's tank is well-fed. _____

WEEK 19 **Wednesday** Name:

Correct these sentences.

1. the cup shood be levil when you pore the punch warned mom

_____

2. i cant beleive i won the jack pot carlos screamed

_____

Write the past tense of the verb *fight*.

3. _____

Singular possessive or plural possessive?

4. the centipede's feet _____

5. the boys' team _____

© Evan-Moor Corp. • Daily Language Review • EMC 576

WEEK 19 **Thursday** Name:

Circle the word that is spelled correctly.

1. tomorow   terible   remember   comeing   hospitel

Write three words with the prefix *mid-*.

2. _____   _____   _____

Correct these sentences.

3. scott came home at 8 30 after the boy scout meeting

_____

4. his friends ask mrs morrow to come to his recitle

_____

Where would the following probably take place?

5. "Would you like to send the package priority? Do the contents need to be insured?"

_____

© Evan-Moor Corp. • Daily Language Review • EMC 576

WEEK 19 Friday

Name:

© Evan-Moor Corp. • Daily Language Review • EMC 576

Combine the sentences to make one sentence.

1. My friends like to go to the gym and work out. I like to go to the gym and work out. We like to go three times a week.

_____

2. Mr. Sutter is my coach. He believes that practice is the key to winning.

_____

3. This morning, the bushes wore new coats of white. There was a snowstorm last night.

_____

4. I called my grandma on the phone. When she first began talking, she sounded weak and shaky. By the time we hung up, her voice was full of life.

_____

5. Mowing the lawn is a big job. Besides cutting the grass, you have to service the mower. Then you have to edge the sidewalk.

_____

WEEK 19 My Progress

Name:

How many did you get correct each day? Color the squares.

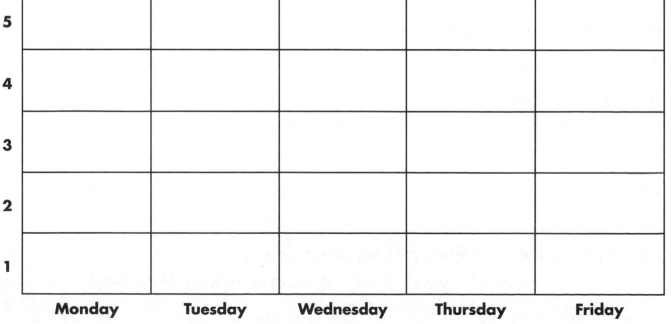

	Monday	Tuesday	Wednesday	Thursday	Friday
5					
4					
3					
2					
1					

© Evan-Moor Corp. • Daily Language Review • EMC 576

WEEK 20 Monday

Name:

Circle the word in which the apostrophe is not used correctly.

1. we'll   mightn't   she'll   has'nt   those'll

Correct these sentences.

2. on friday my frends and I will go two central zoo sad sue

_____

3. "peter wood you rather sea the tigger the lion or the chimp"

_____

What function do the underlined words in this sentence have?

4. The Mayans may <u>have transported</u> stones over long distances when they built their temples.

_____

Write the plural form of this noun.

5. tomato _____

WEEK 20 Tuesday

Name:

Simile or metaphor?

1. The baby's hair was corn silk against her soft pink face. _____

Circle the word that is not spelled correctly.

2. guessed   enough   supposed   poison   insted

Correct these sentences.

3. there weding cayk was sew tall it almost reached the sealing

_____

4. the brides vale borrowed from her aunt lookt like a shiney cloud

_____

Use context clues to determine the meaning of the bolded word.

5. Everyone brought something to eat, so we had a **bountiful** amount of food for the potluck.

_____

WEEK 20 Wednesday

Name:

Correct these sentences.

1. in my room ive displayt mi collecktion of caps from evry baseball team

_____

2. its fun to wear one and amagine your self at bat facing randy johnson

_____

What print reference source would you use to find the street address of your local pizza parlor?

3. _____

What does the abbreviation _misc._ stand for?

4. _____

Circle the cause and underline the effect.

5. When Thutmose II died, his son was too young to assume the responsibilities of a pharaoh, so his wife Hatshepsut became pharaoh instead.

WEEK 20 Thursday

Name:

Circle the word that comes last in alphabetical order.

1. disprove   dissatisfy   dissolute   dissent   dissection

Write a homophone for the word _piece_.

2. _____

Correct these sentences.

3. my uncle one the distinguished flying cross for his bravry

_____

4. were all very prowd of hiz specil distincshun

_____

Circle the words that are adverbs.

5. pretty   there   swam   softly   until

WEEK 20 Friday

Name:

© Evan-Moor Corp. • Daily Language Review • EMC 576

What do the underlined phrases mean?

1. Thomas <u>lost his temper</u> for no reason.

_____

2. I <u>got cold feet</u> when it came time to <u>take the stage</u>.

_____

3. I can't go to the game today, but I'll <u>take a rain check</u>.

_____

4. Sadi bought the used computer game <u>for a song</u>.

_____

5. She was <u>skating on thin ice</u> when she stepped over the guardrail to take a photograph.

_____

WEEK 20 My Progress

Name:

© Evan-Moor Corp. • Daily Language Review • EMC 576

How many did you get correct each day? Color the squares.

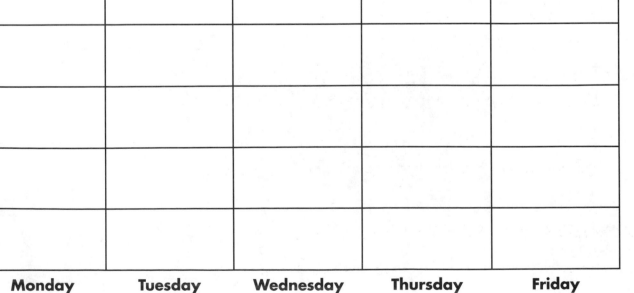

	Monday	Tuesday	Wednesday	Thursday	Friday
5					
4					
3					
2					
1					

Monday

Name:

Correct these sentences.

1. can you come over to watch *jeopardy* asked jamal

_____

2. my mom is out of town so ill ask grandpa travis answered

_____

Circle the cause and underline the effect.

3. Archaeologists believe that around 1400 B.C., some great disaster struck the palace at Knossos; they found smoke stains on the walls, as well as scattered vessels.

Circle the best word to complete this sentence.

4. Steven has _____ three inches in the last six months.

   groan   grown

Circle the antonyms in this sentence.

5. If you do a thorough job of research, you will find that writing a conclusion is much easier than if you do an incomplete job and don't understand your subject.

Tuesday

Name:

Choose the best word to complete this sentence.

1. It's my job to make sure that the floor has been _____.

   sweeped   sweped   swept   swepted

Circle the words that have the same sound as /ow/ in *now*.

2. couch   allow   throw   house   trout   bough

Correct these sentences.

3. teresa will pick-up the papers sweep and dust

_____

4. what dew you want too be responsibul four ask mrs timms

_____

Fact or fantasy?

5. When the water evaporated, it became invisible vapor. _____

WEEK 21 **Wednesday**   Name:

Correct these sentences.

1. them players choosed mr rupp as the best basket ball couch

_____

2. hav you every heared the beatles song yellow submarine

_____

What is the present tense of the verb _spoke_?

3. _____

If the guide words on a dictionary page are _stringent_ and _structure_, which words would not be on the page?

4. string   stripe   strong   stroke   struggle   strident

Choose the best word to complete this analogy.

5. _Fish_ are to _creel_ as _strawberries_ are to _____.
   shortcake   pudding   basket   field

WEEK 21 **Thursday**   Name:

What is the object of this sentence?

1. Grandma bought Whitney a puzzle with over 1,000 pieces. _____

Where is someone who sees the following?

2. The captains meet at midfield for the coin toss before the kickoff.

_____

Correct these sentences.

3. sydeny asked will we sea sharks at ocean world

_____

4. after school I saw peter who asked can you stop buy my house

_____

Write the root or base word.

5. contradiction _____

© Evan-Moor Corp. • Daily Language Review • EMC 576

Choose the best word to complete each sentence.

1. He _____ seen walking by the pond yesterday.
   is   been   was

2. When _____ you think you will finish the book report?
   does   do   don't

3. Bill, please give this cup of tea to _____.
   him   them   he

4. How many _____ were exhibited at the fair?
   sheep   sheeps   sheep's   sheepes

5. _____ going to the ballgame?
   Whose   Who's   Who   Whom

How many did you get correct each day? Color the squares.

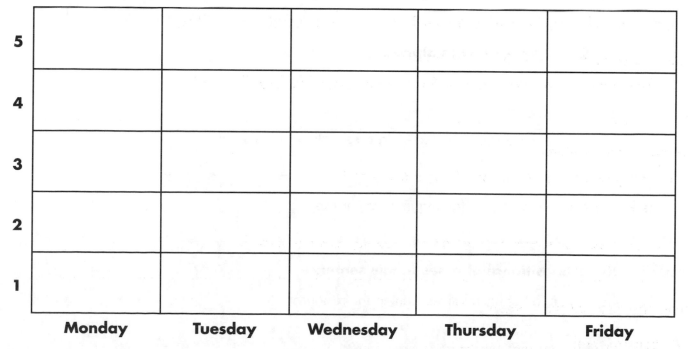

	Monday	Tuesday	Wednesday	Thursday	Friday
5					
4					
3					
2					
1					

© Evan-Moor Corp. • Daily Language Review • EMC 576

WEEK 22 Monday

Name:

Correct these sentences.

1. josh tori and maddie went to disney world

_____

2. thay road space mountain rock 'n' roller coaster and test track

_____

Use context clues to determine the meaning of the bolded word.

3. Jeremy took some time to **contemplate** the question before he answered it.

_____

Circle the words that are spelled correctly.

4. manufacture   volenteer   charecteristic   civilization   infectted

Is the underlined word singular possessive or plural possessive?

5. The women's room is down the hall. _____

WEEK 22 Tuesday

Name:

Circle the adjectives in this sentence.

1. Mouth-watering aromas seeped from Mother's oven and made my hungry stomach rumble.

Circle the word that comes last in alphabetical order.

2. guava   guest   guardsman   guise   guile

Correct these sentences.

3. if you join the book club you will recieve a prescription to *highlights*

_____

4. perks supreme is the only koffee that my mother like

_____

Underline the prepositional phrases in this sentence.

5. After the service, all of his relatives went to the restaurant.

© Evan-Moor Corp. • Daily Language Review • EMC 576

WEEK 22 Wednesday

Name: _____

Correct these sentences.

1. if we go to study hall now dave boasted well be finished first

   _____

2. huck finn is a ficshunel charactr created by mark twain

   _____

Write the correct abbreviation for *September*.

3. _____

Rewrite this word, adding a suffix.

4. state   _____

What is the subject of this sentence?

5. Will you be able to get your homework done on time?   _____

WEEK 22 Thursday

Name: _____

Write synonyms and antonyms for these words.

1. accurate   Synonym: _____   Antonym: _____

2. glamorous   Synonym: _____   Antonym: _____

Correct these sentences.

3. meekers student council voted to visit hospitals on thanksgiving

   _____

4. the teachers will go two ralphs to by the food

   _____

Divide this word into syllables.

5. mosquito   _____

WEEK
22 **Friday**

Name:

Label the subject and verb or verbs in each sentence.

1. Ted's puppy wagged its tail and barked.

    Subject: _____   Verb(s): _____

2. Slippery Rock is the name of a town.

    Subject: _____   Verb(s): _____

3. The squirrel gathered nuts and stored them in its cheeks.

    Subject: _____   Verb(s): _____

4. How did you do on the test?

    Subject: _____   Verb(s): _____

5. Summer vacation is almost here.

    Subject: _____   Verb(s): _____

© Evan-Moor Corp. • Daily Language Review • EMC 576

WEEK
22 **My Progress**

Name:

How many did you get correct each day? Color the squares.

	Monday	Tuesday	Wednesday	Thursday	Friday
5					
4					
3					
2					
1					

© Evan-Moor Corp. • Daily Language Review • EMC 576

WEEK 23 Monday

© Evan-Moor Corp. • Daily Language Review • EMC 576

Name:

Correct these sentences.

1. keli and glen want two go horse back riding on friday at 3 o clock

_____

2. the smith twins sara and emily where matching outfites

_____

Write a word that belongs in this group.

3. bang, crash, ping, splash, splat, _____

Past, present, or future?

4. When will you go to camp? _____

Name this part of a business letter.

5. I'm writing to inform you that you've been awarded the contract. _____

WEEK 23 Tuesday

Name:

© Evan-Moor Corp. • Daily Language Review • EMC 576

Choose the best word to complete this sentence.

1. Fred is so tired, he needs to _____ down before the game.

        lay   laid   lie   lying

If the guide words on a dictionary page are *claim* and *classical*, which words would be on the page?

2. clatter   classroom   clasp   clarinet   clack   clam

Correct these sentences.

3. when im tried of writeing i stand up and breath deeply

_____

4. often what i think i key board is not whats on the page

_____

Synonyms or antonyms?

5. endure, persist _____

WEEK 23

Wednesday

Name: _____

Correct these sentences.

1. when i asked who is it i heard a voice replie its only me

_____

2. humpty dumpty posed a impossible challenge for the kings mens

_____

Write a fact about *homework*.

3. _____

Circle the two pairs of synonyms in this sentence.

4. I hope to locate the original deed or to at least discover the first owner's name.

Does the underlined adverb phrase tell how, when, where, or to what extent?

5. The jukebox played the song <u>over and over.</u> _____

WEEK 23

Thursday

Name: _____

Write the possessive noun.

1. the three dogs of Arturo _____

Use context clues to determine the meaning of the bolded word.

2. Although we can live a long time without food, water is **indispensable**.

_____

Correct these sentences.

3. its all most lunch time shouted simon

_____

4. hurry lets go to carpenter beach four a piknic

_____

Does the underlined adjective tell which ones, what kind, or how many?

5. <u>Those</u> wiggly worms felt funny in my hand. _____

WEEK 23 Friday

Name:

© Evan-Moor Corp. • Daily Language Review • EMC 576

Read the following paragraph and decide if the underlined parts have a capitalization error, a punctuation error, a spelling error, or no error.

Have you ever wondered where ice cream came from. On one of his trips to the Far East,

<u>1</u>   <u>2</u>

Marco Polo returned to italy with a recipe for a frozen milk desert. Italy is credited with

<u>3</u>   <u>4</u>

popularising ice cream.

<u>5</u>

1. _____

2. _____

3. _____

4. _____

5. _____

WEEK 23 My Progress

Name:

How many did you get correct each day? Color the squares.

5				
4				
3				
2				
1				
Monday	**Tuesday**	**Wednesday**	**Thursday**	**Friday**

© Evan-Moor Corp. • Daily Language Review • EMC 576

WEEK 24 Monday

Name:

© Evan-Moor Corp. • Daily Language Review • EMC 576

Correct these sentences.

1. of all the stars in the sky the sun is the closer to earth

_____

2. its a bawl of burning gas's thats about fiv billion years old

_____

Does the underlined adverb tell how, when, where, or to what extent?

3. Tori liked to twist her hair and pin it <u>up</u> in a knot. _____

Simile or metaphor?

4. Mrs. Perch's hair was a nest for the perky red bow. _____

Is the underlined word singular or plural?

5. Which <u>fish</u> in the aquarium swims the fastest? _____

WEEK 24 Tuesday

Name:

© Evan-Moor Corp. • Daily Language Review • EMC 576

Is the bolded word a subject pronoun or an object pronoun?

1. We wanted to thank **them** for all of their help. _____

Correct these sentences.

2. do you think that some day sum one will travel all the weigh to mars

_____

3. sid nose that the letter was supposd to arived on june 10 by 10 a m

_____

What is the meaning of this figure of speech?

4. Nancy always <u>has her nose in a book.</u> _____

Circle the subject of this sentence.

5. Covered with suds and dripping with water, the toddler dashed from the bathtub to the bedroom.

WEEK 24 Wednesday

Name: _____

Correct these sentences.

1. youd beter clean up that mess quick

_____

2. boris and jean packt the picters for the air express truck

_____

Choose the best word to complete this sentence.

3. Scott had _____ many dirty dishes in his room.

      two   to   too   tow

Write *sentence* or *not a sentence* on the line.

4. Always busy working in the kitchen, the cooks _____

5. The computer responded to his command _____

WEEK 24 Thursday

Name: _____

Circle the contraction that is spelled correctly.

1. we'll   there'ell   they'are   that'ill   ther'ed

Which part of speech is underlined: noun, verb, adjective, or adverb?

2. The runner sprinted down the track <u>effortlessly</u>. _____

Correct these sentences.

3. in his poem primer lesson carl sandburg wrote look out how you use proud words

_____

4. isnt it all most time for the asembly

_____

Synonyms or antonyms?

5. tumult, pandemonium _____

WEEK 24 Friday   Name:

Combine the sentences to make one sentence.

1. Marilyn bought some sandals. She tried on hiking boots, walking shoes, and ballet slippers.

_____

2. We drove to the camping store to buy a tent cover. When we got there, the store was closed.

_____

3. The road was covered with black ice. The car turned the corner. The car slid off the road.

_____

4. Jo went to visit her sister. Jo's sister lives in St. Louis. Jo only has one sister.

_____

5. I found a carton of eggs in the refrigerator. It had only one egg in it. I couldn't make cookies.

_____

© Evan-Moor Corp. • Daily Language Review • EMC 576

WEEK 24 My Progress   Name:

How many did you get correct each day? Color the squares.

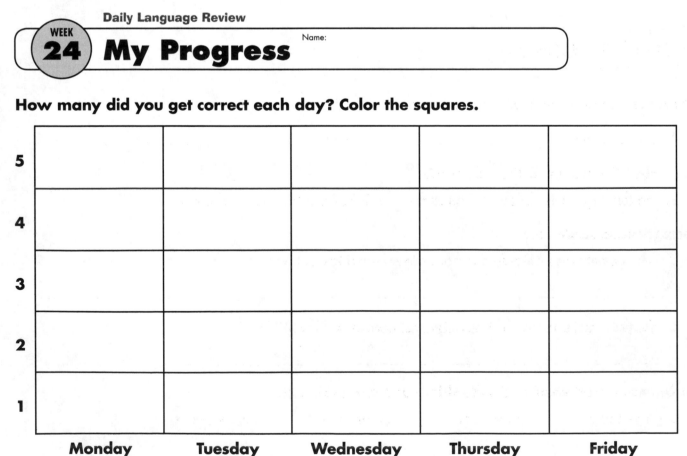

	Monday	Tuesday	Wednesday	Thursday	Friday
5					
4					
3					
2					
1					

© Evan-Moor Corp. • Daily Language Review • EMC 576

WEEK 25 **Monday**

Name:

Correct these sentences.

1. these here sentenses our begining to all look a like

_____

2. honey is a treet four bares sayed the zoo keaper

_____

Write the possessive noun.

3. the books of the teachers _____

Use this homophone pair in one sentence: _plain, plane._

4. _____

Fact or opinion?

5. A brainstorm is a good idea. _____

WEEK 25 **Tuesday**

Name:

Write the comparative and superlative forms of _quiet._

1. Comparative: _____ Superlative: _____

Underline the nouns in this sentence.

2. The kindergartners buzzed around the soccer ball like bees around a hive.

Correct these sentences.

3. i use post it notes to lable the paiges that kneed korrections

_____

4. after ten laps around the track his chest heaves as he breaths

_____

Circle the correct way to divide this word into syllables.

5. en ve lop e   en vel ope   en ve lope   env el ope

WEEK 25 Wednesday

Name:

© Evan-Moor Corp. • Daily Language Review • EMC 576

Correct these sentences.

1. my gardner suggests i planted tulips lilacs and a rose

_____

2. hav you had two hav you're teeth pulled buy a dentist

_____

Choose the best word to complete this analogy.

3. *Seldom* is to *often* as *many* is to _____.
   lots   more   few   several

Suffix or prefix?

4. envious   _____

5. entrust   _____

WEEK 25 Thursday

Name:

© Evan-Moor Corp. • Daily Language Review • EMC 576

Circle the cause and underline the effect.

1. To avoid the extreme daytime heat, we drove across the desert at night.

What print reference source would you use to find a synonym for *length*?

2. _____

Correct these sentences.

3. i bought kiwi from mexico and pinapple from hawaii

_____

4. can you git some peeches for me ask frank

_____

Choose the correct date to complete this sentence.

5. Mrs. Ford was born on _____ at Weld County General Hospital.
   March 13 1982   March 13, 1982   March 13, 1982,

WEEK 25 Friday

Name: _____

© Evan-Moor Corp. • Daily Language Review • EMC 576

Write what the underlined phrases mean.

1. <u>Let's get down to brass tacks.</u> How much do you want for your bike?

   _____

2. My mom <u>gets a kick out of</u> shopping.

   _____

3. I don't believe the salesman. He's <u>full of hot air.</u>

   _____

4. On the soccer field, I feel <u>like a fish out of water.</u>

   _____

5. His idea to start school fifteen minutes earlier every day <u>went over like a lead balloon.</u>

   _____

WEEK 25 My Progress

Name: _____

How many did you get correct each day? Color the squares.

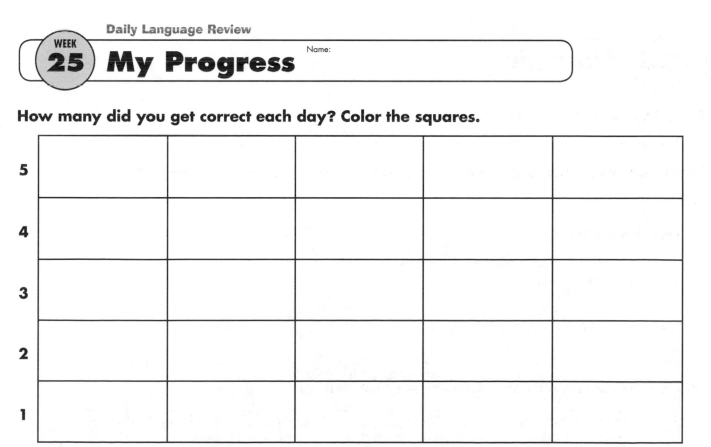

	Monday	Tuesday	Wednesday	Thursday	Friday
5					
4					
3					
2					
1					

© Evan-Moor Corp. • Daily Language Review • EMC 576

WEEK 26 **Monday**

Name:

Correct these sentences.

1. ray will pick up his new pick up at truck city tomorow

_____

2. during the last rain storm my roof sprung a leak

_____

Use the context clues to determine the meaning of the bolded word.

3. Kali's **charisma** made her a popular choice for class president.

_____

Identify this part of a friendly letter.

4. Dear Aunt Betty, _____

Underline the prepositional phrase in this sentence.

5. My baby sister sits in her highchair, giggles, and throws her food overboard.

WEEK 26 **Tuesday**

Name:

Circle the correct abbreviation for *quart*.

1. qrt.   q.   qt.   QT

Write a proper noun for each common noun.

2. city _____

3. business _____

Correct these sentences.

4. the scott boys bike club meets on wedesday after skhool

_____

5. wood you like to come to the next meating as my gest

_____

WEEK 26 **Wednesday**   Name: _____

Correct these sentences.

1. when beavers built dams everie member of an beaver family helps

_____

2. mother father and three or for younger beavers work togather

_____

Write the comparative and superlative adjectives of *easy*.

3. Comparative: _____   Superlative: _____

Choose the best word to complete this analogy.

4. password : computer network :: key : _____
   house   lock   ring   mouse

Write the complete subject of this sentence.

5. The transparent plastic crate held all of her photos and letters.

_____

WEEK 26 **Thursday**   Name: _____

Write the pronouns that would replace the underlined nouns.

<u>Megan and Chelsea</u> played on the <u>trampoline</u>.
       1   **2**

1. _____

2. _____

Correct these sentences.

3. they're many diffrent kinds of letus lik romaine and bibb

_____

4. chef dennis uses for lettuce's in his famose harvest salad

_____

Circle the cause and underline the effect.

5. Don watched a DVD on my dad's computer, so when Dad turned it on, the battery was low.

WEEK 26 Friday

Name: _____

Circle the best word to complete each sentence.

1. Tommy looked all over for the keys he _____.

                               lose   losed   lost

2. Samantha _____ all the Girl Scouts her new badge.

          show   shown   showed

3. Did you know _____ both from Nebraska?

        their   they're   there

4. Why did you _____ those cookies so close to suppertime?

        eat   ate   eaten

5. The choir had _____ the school song at the assembly.

        sang   singed   sung

© Evan-Moor Corp. • Daily Language Review • EMC 576

WEEK 26 My Progress

Name: _____

How many did you get correct each day? Color the squares.

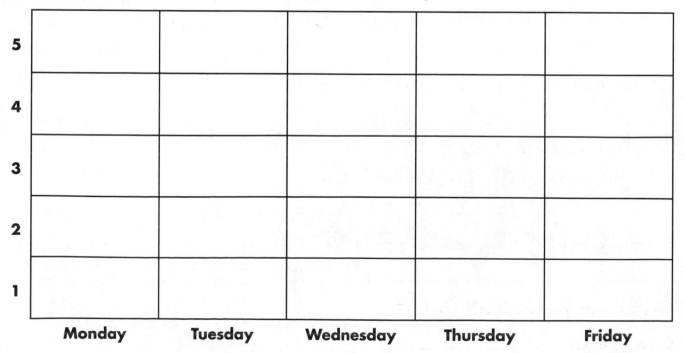

	Monday	Tuesday	Wednesday	Thursday	Friday
5					
4					
3					
2					
1					

© Evan-Moor Corp. • Daily Language Review • EMC 576

WEEK 27 Monday Name:

© Evan-Moor Corp. • Daily Language Review • EMC 576

Correct these sentences.

1. i named my pet george because i got him at georges pet store

_____

2. when i pet georges i says youre my bestest frend

_____

Is the bolded word a subject pronoun or an object pronoun?

3. Will **you** dance with Mary at the recital? _____

4. Can you eat **it** and play at the same time? _____

What do these words have in common?

5. knit   crochet   cross-stitch   needlepoint

_____

WEEK 27 Tuesday Name:

© Evan-Moor Corp. • Daily Language Review • EMC 576

What part of speech is underlined in these sentences?

1. The narrow road <u>twisted</u> between the tall, snowy mountains.

_____

2. <u>Twenty-five</u> team members competed in the tournament.

_____

Correct these sentences.

3. the navajo people are famos for there beutiful rugs

_____

4. historyical thay livd on the southwestern planes

_____

Synonyms, antonyms, or homophones?

5. moan, mown _____

WEEK 27 Wednesday

Name: _____

Correct these sentences.

1. Pete finded his faverit dvd transformers under hiz bed

_____

2. dr morgan xrayed annies teeth and said no cavitys

_____

Rewrite the word *graph*, adding a prefix.

3. _____

Where would the following probably take place?

4. "Don't forget to write your name on your test. Show all your work."

_____

Circle the two words that need to be switched in order to make the list in correct alphabetical order.

5. stoke   stole   stomach   stoop   stone

WEEK 27 Thursday

Name: _____

Circle the word that is a plural noun.

1. people   dog's   dress   goes

Correct these sentences.

2. the trafik wasn't bad this mourning maybe its a holiday

_____

3. frank complained my hands are chap becuz of the cold wet whether

_____

Write the past and future tenses of the verb *forbid*.

4. Past: _____   Future: _____

Circle the complete subject of this sentence.

5. The enormous elephants, two fierce tigers, a gawky llama, and Bobo the trained bear shared the train car with the Flying Delaneys—all twelve of them!

© Evan-Moor Corp. • Daily Language Review • EMC 576

WEEK 27 Friday

Name: _____

© Evan-Moor Corp. • Daily Language Review • EMC 576

Complete each sentence, using the appropriate homophones.

(hole, whole)
1. Philip spent the _____ morning mending a _____ in his sock.

(right, write)
2. Be sure that you _____ the _____ answer for each question.

(principal, principle)
3. I set up a meeting with the _____ because I believed that the basic _____ behind the code had been violated.

(raise, raze, rays)
4. Through the bright _____ of first morning, the soldier began to _____ the new flag. At the same time, the bulldozers began to _____ the old building.

(stationery, stationary)
5. With plumed pen and embossed _____, the scribe assumed her _____ position for the diorama.

WEEK 27 My Progress

Name: _____

© Evan-Moor Corp. • Daily Language Review • EMC 576

How many did you get correct each day? Color the squares.

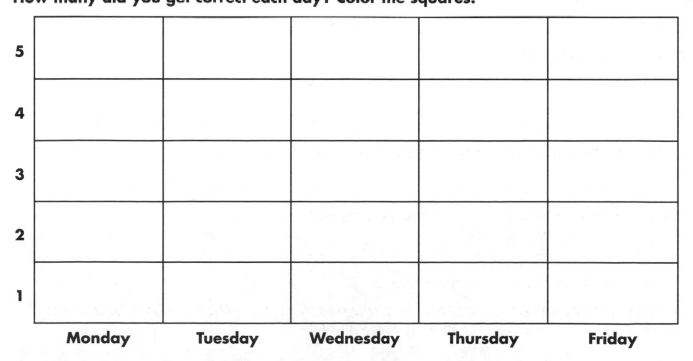

	Monday	Tuesday	Wednesday	Thursday	Friday
5					
4					
3					
2					
1					

WEEK 28 Monday

Name: _____

Correct these sentences.

1. heather weaved a small blanket for the babies bed

_____

2. drew knew the write anser befor the teecher had ask the queston

_____

Use the context clues to determine the meaning of the bolded word.

3. I was **enthralled** by the book and read nonstop for hours.

_____

Write the root or base word.

4. reconstruction _____

5. imported _____

WEEK 28 Tuesday

Name: _____

Circle the correct way to divide this word into syllables.

1. lum in ous   lu min ous   lu mi nous   lum i nous

Correct these sentences.

2. the ladie wavved her hand at her reltor and said we want that house

_____

3. the house was desihnd by a famus archtekt named frank lloyd wright

_____

Are the underlined words the subject or the predicate?

4. When evening came, the bubbling brook's babble seemed to increase in volume.

_____

The word *reflection* has _____.

5. a prefix   a suffix   both a prefix and a suffix   neither a prefix nor a suffix

© Evan-Moor Corp. • Daily Language Review • EMC 576

WEEK 28

Wednesday

Name: _____

© Evan-Moor Corp. • Daily Language Review • EMC 576

Correct these sentences.

1. mr gerk announcd if i don't have coffey my day is off too a bad start

_____

2. here sir said hillary i think i can help as she heald out a steeming mug

_____

Fact or opinion?

3. All students need foreign language training. _____

Correct the spelling of the words that are not spelled correctly.

4. athletes   chocolotes   rhythems   purchases

_____

Circle the words that are adverbs.

5. suddenly   regrettably   hustle   soon   significant

WEEK 28

Thursday

Name: _____

© Evan-Moor Corp. • Daily Language Review • EMC 576

Does the underlined adjective tell which one, what kind, or how many?

1. <u>Summer</u> days are barefoot walks in cool grass. _____

2. <u>Those</u> mosquitoes love summer days, too. _____

Correct these sentences.

3. run six laps before comeing too class coach okeefe said

_____

4. thirdy two differnt speeshes of birds live near lake oswego

_____

Simile or metaphor?

5. Rain is a magic elixir that changes brown landscape to green. _____

WEEK 28 Friday

Name:

Read the following paragraph and decide if the underlined parts have a capitalization error, a punctuation error, a spelling error, or no error.

Tomas huddled <u>like a scarred animal</u> in the brush. He had come to <u>this region to give a lecture</u>
          1   **2**

about using plants from the <u>amazon rainforest</u> for medical research, but now he was stranded
                               3

on <u>a deserted unpaved</u> road <u>somewhere near the equator.</u>
      4   **5**

1. _____

2. _____

3. _____

4. _____

5. _____

WEEK 28 My Progress

Name:

How many did you get correct each day? Color the squares.

	Monday	Tuesday	Wednesday	Thursday	Friday
5					
4					
3					
2					
1					

© Evan-Moor Corp. • Daily Language Review • EMC 576

WEEK 29 Monday

Name:

Correct these sentences.

1. molly and max his two terriers make life exciting at joshs house

_____

2. we read the declartion of independance in hour class

_____

Write the comparative and superlative forms of *bad.*

3. Comparative: _____ Superlative: _____

Is it a sentence? Circle *yes* or *no.*

4. Ted at the wheel, the blue van piled with gifts for all the cousins   yes   no

5. Come here   yes   no

WEEK 29 Tuesday

Name:

Circle the cause and underline the effect.

1. Forest Service officials are combing the area for Japanese Beetle larvae. Last week, the larvae were found in a backyard garden. They are considered a danger to area vineyards.

Correct these sentences.

2. stuart little is a carring new comer to the little family

_____

3. nashvil tennessee is the capitol of that state

_____

Write the appropriate word in each sentence: *leased, least.*

4. He _____ the garage for the upcoming year.

5. Having a roof over his head was the _____ of his worries.

EMC 576

© Evan-Moor Corp. • Daily Language Review • EMC 576

WEEK 29 **Wednesday**

Name:

Correct these sentences.

1. a trip to the museum of natrual history is a treet exclaimed sara

_____

2. tomorow is my favorit song from annie

_____

What is this part of a business letter called?

3. Sincerely,

   Tom Adams, Secretary _____

Underline the prepositional phrases in this sentence.

4. In this helter-skelter world, I need to find a place of my own quickly.

Complete this analogy.

5. foundation : cement :: skeleton : _____

WEEK 29 **Thursday**

Name:

Circle the correct abbreviation for *District of Columbia*.

1. Dist. of Co.   D of C   D.C.   DC

Declarative, interrogative, imperative, or exclamatory?

2. Give Sam a hand for his effort. _____

Correct these sentences.

3. imagin a arbor with roses cascading frum it's branchs

_____

4. my garden is lik a vegetbul stand with dayly prodeuce spechuls

_____

Circle the correct way to divide this word into syllables.

5. hea vi er   heav i er   heav ier   hea vie r

WEEK 29 Friday

Name:

Label the subject and verb in each sentence.

1. Pat and Mike went fishing.

   Subject: _____   Verb: _____

2. Mike brought the fishing poles.

   Subject: _____   Verb: _____

3. Pat caught the first fish.

   Subject: _____   Verb: _____

4. The fish was too small to keep.

   Subject: _____   Verb: _____

5. He threw the tiny fish back into the water.

   Subject: _____   Verb: _____

© Evan-Moor Corp. • Daily Language Review • EMC 576

WEEK 29 My Progress

Name:

How many did you get correct each day? Color the squares.

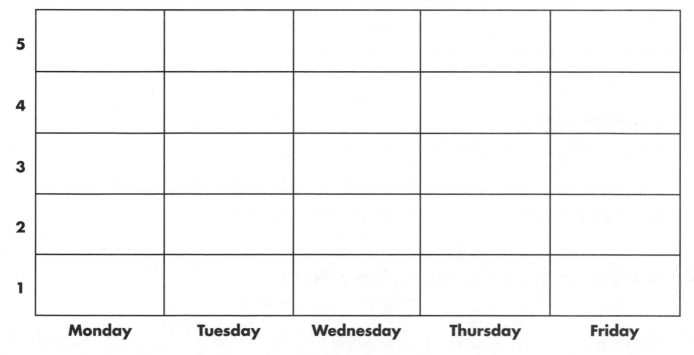

	Monday	Tuesday	Wednesday	Thursday	Friday
5					
4					
3					
2					
1					

© Evan-Moor Corp. • Daily Language Review • EMC 576

WEEK 30 **Monday**

Name:

Correct these sentences.

1. jose finded a wallet with recepts from a account at world bank

_____

2. when he returnned the wallet to securitie he recieved a reward of 50 dollars

_____

Use the context clues to determine the meaning of the bolded word.

3. The escaping robber was **encumbered** by the heavy sack of loot.

_____

Past, present, or future?

4. Patricia can't wait for her birthday party. _____

5. Walking in the forest provided a respite in Bob's day. _____

WEEK 30 **Tuesday**

Name:

Fact or opinion?

1. My piano teacher can play ragtime melodies with flair. _____

Write an antonym for the word *optimistic*.

2. _____

Correct these sentences.

3. dr lee is a pediatrician who is like a grandfather to his patience

_____

4. why didnt julie take drivers education this summer

_____

Use this homophone pair in one sentence: *scent, sent*.

5. _____

WEEK 30 Wednesday Name:

Correct these sentences.

1. mr smith the art teacher lended me the book about picasso

   _____

2. peter and me want to try to pant a murel in picassos style

   _____

Is the underlined word a noun, verb, adjective, or adverb?

3. A threatening cloud <u>hung</u> high in the sky as we anticipated rain. _____

Circle the word that is spelled correctly.

4. weapen   secend   hospitel   happen

Does the underlined adjective tell which one, what kind, or how many?

5. <u>Shimmering</u> stars shine softly in the summer sky. _____

WEEK 30 Thursday Name:

Past, present, or future?

1. The farmer is having a sale of his farm equipment in the fall. _____

2. Colby flew to Amsterdam for Petrov's graduation. _____

Correct these sentences.

3. noises especially loud ones are frightening at night explained fred

   _____

4. my kitten ollie naps wakes up and stretches and than sleeps sum more

   _____

Write the comparative and superlative adjectives of *funny*.

5. Comparative: _____   Superlative: _____

WEEK 30 Friday

Name: _____

Write the letter of the meaning for each underlined word or words.

1. The police officer may <u>cite</u> you for speeding. _____

2. It was a magnificent <u>sight</u>! _____

3. Our school is to be the <u>site</u> of the filming. _____

4. The <u>sight</u> on the telescope helps the astronomer. _____

5. The boy <u>set his sights on</u> winning the trophy. _____

a. to strive for
b. a device looked through to help aim
c. summon to court
d. display
e. location

WEEK 30 My Progress

Name: _____

How many did you get correct each day? Color the squares.

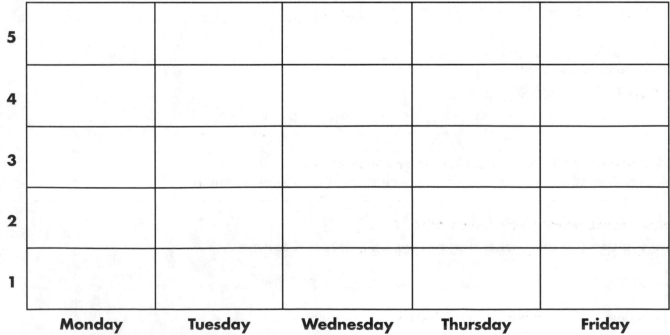

	Monday	Tuesday	Wednesday	Thursday	Friday
5					
4					
3					
2					
1					

WEEK 31 Monday

Name:

Correct these sentences.

1. the pioneer society is a group of descendints of familys that home steaded in the west

_____

2. my grate grandmothers parents were part of that originel settlment

_____

Write synonyms for these words.

3. retrieve _____

4. secluded _____

Does the underlined adverb tell when, how much, or where?

5. The doctor showed patience as the traffic crawled <u>forward.</u>

_____

WEEK 31 Tuesday

Name:

What is the meaning of this figure of speech?

1. I've got a big test tomorrow. I'd better <u>hit the books.</u>

_____

Correct these sentences.

2. how many of there are us

_____

3. sal and ron and me went out to hour new club house

_____

What do these words have in common?

4. spaghetti   linguine   manicotti   ziti

_____

5. diapers   stroller   bottles   bib

Correct these sentences.

1. my little couzen always says give me 5

_____

2. the phone rung jest as mom was leafing the house

_____

Circle the cause and underline the effect.

3. I missed my connection in Denver due to a late takeoff in Los Angeles.

Write an opinion about *violence*.

4. _____

Circle the word that is not spelled correctly.

5. authoritative   fragmentary   presentible   fractional   prejudice

© Evan-Moor Corp. • Daily Language Review • EMC 576

What type of job is described here?

1. He carefully checked the network organization and then installed the new hub.

_____

Use context clues to determine the meaning of the bolded word.

2. Sugar is an **essential** ingredient in making sugar cookies.

_____

Correct these sentences.

3. i just finished reding a book entitled through my eyes by ruby bridges

_____

4. it descrbed her experience as the only black student in her school

_____

Underline the complete predicate of this sentence.

5. After the false start, the swimmer dove into the water and swam to victory.

© Evan-Moor Corp. • Daily Language Review • EMC 576

WEEK 31 Friday

Name:

Read the following paragraph and decide if the underlined parts have a capitalization error, a punctuation error, a spelling error, or no error.

Success in reading depends on using active strategies to <u>increase comprihension.</u> <u>Do you have</u>
1 2

<u>stratedgies that you use.</u> Before you read, do you organize your materials and tune in
3

to the task? <u>As you read do you take notes and</u> look up words? <u>After you read do you</u>
4 5

review and use your new information to answer questions?

1. _____

2. _____

3. _____

4. _____

5. _____

WEEK 31 My Progress

Name:

How many did you get correct each day? Color the squares.

	Monday	Tuesday	Wednesday	Thursday	Friday
5					
4					
3					
2					
1					

WEEK 32 Monday

Name:

Correct these sentences.

1. pebbles and bam bam are charesters in the movie the flint stones

_____

2. because it snowd mr ruiz the building manager cleared the walks

_____

Simile or metaphor?

3. The quiet surrounded her like a soft, downy comforter. _____

Circle the word that is not spelled correctly.

4. feeling   group   makings   natcheral   quarrelsome

What time is it?

5. The clock in the hallway chimed one, but there was no one about, and even the stars seemed

to sleep under a thick blanket of clouds. _____

WEEK 32 Tuesday

Name:

Write the possessive form.

1. uniforms of those band members   _____

Correct these sentences.

2. homer spit is a peace of land that juts into kamishak bay from alaska

_____

3. the empress hotel in victoria british columbia has a lovey dinning room

_____

Synonyms, antonyms, or homophones?

4. pair, pare   _____

Number these words in the correct alphabetical order.

5. ☐ breakage   ☐ breadwinner   ☐ breeze   ☐ brevity   ☐ breakfast

WEEK 32 Wednesday

Name:

Correct these sentences.

1. me and my brothers like to play monopoly on saturday after noons

   _____

2. eating a apple every day is suppose to keep the docter away

   _____

Write the two words that make up this contraction.

3. would've _____ _____

What part of speech is underlined in this sentence?

4. <u>Avoid</u> eating too many sweets. _____

Circle the word that does not belong.

5. plywood   oak   maple   birch   elm

WEEK 32 Thursday

Name:

Use this homophone pair in one sentence: *gate, gait*.

1. _____

If the guide words on a dictionary page are *dabble* and *damage*, which words would not be found on the page?

2. Dalmatian   dainty   dab   damask   daily

Correct these sentences.

3. once up on a time there was a king and a queen and a magnificant castel

   _____

4. pleeze put up you're umbrela after your out side the door

   _____

Rewrite the word *bank*, adding a prefix and a suffix.

5. _____

© Evan-Moor Corp. • Daily Language Review • EMC 576

WEEK 32 Friday

Name:

Complete these sentences.

1. The best book I ever read was _____.

2. _____ is my favorite song of all time.

3. _____ was the best movie I saw this year.

4. I could read the poem _____ over and over again.

5. Yesterday, I watched _____ on television.

WEEK 32 My Progress

Name:

© Evan-Moor Corp. • Daily Language Review • EMC 576

How many did you get correct each day? Color the squares.

	Monday	Tuesday	Wednesday	Thursday	Friday
5					
4					
3					
2					
1					

Correct these sentences.

1. i use choclate bars marshmellows and crackers to make a tastey desert

_____

2. the name of the deserts s'mores and you will want more after you're furst one

_____

Write the base or root word.

3. standardization _____

4. conspiracy _____

Underline the adverb phrase in this sentence.

5. Take what she says with a grain of salt.

© Evan-Moor Corp. • Daily Language Review • EMC 576

Circle the complete predicate in this sentence.

1. Did Max snore last night?

Use context clues to determine the meaning of the bolded word.

2. The **vain** actor kept photos of himself all over the house.

_____

Correct these sentences.

3. i believe that goldilocks was a trespaser announced the teacher

_____

4. I agree with you're assessment replyed the student

_____

Rewrite the word _scope_, adding a prefix.

5. _____

© Evan-Moor Corp. • Daily Language Review • EMC 576

WEEK 33 **Wednesday**

Name: _____

© Evan-Moor Corp. • Daily Language Review • EMC 576

Correct these sentences.

1. black widow spiders and mexican tarantula are faresome insexts

_____

2. some times I wish I was a eagle soring threw the clear blew sky

_____

Complete this analogy.

3. predator : prey :: lion : _____

What part of speech is the underlined word?

4. Suddenly the wind burst through the window and <u>slapped</u> the door closed.

_____

5. When the mouse ran <u>across</u> the room, Carolyn stood on a chair and screamed.

_____

WEEK 33 **Thursday**

Name: _____

© Evan-Moor Corp. • Daily Language Review • EMC 576

Write the pronoun that would replace the underlined nouns in this sentence.

1. I mixed <u>carrots, peas, and mushrooms</u> in the pan. _____

Circle the word that does not belong in this group.

2. vertical   horizontal   square   perpendicular   parallel

Correct these sentences.

3. tonya said my legs go two sleep when i set on them

_____

4. stephen said oh my legs go too sleep when im laying on the bed

_____

What part of speech is the underlined word?

5. The books were <u>so</u> heavy that I almost dropped them. _____

WEEK
33 **Friday**

Name:

What do the underlined phrases mean?

1. When Scott sees my new bike, he'll be <u>green with envy.</u>

_____

2. When it comes to swimming, Tony is <u>head and shoulders above</u> everyone else.

_____

3. The coach thinks that the game is <u>in the bag.</u>

_____

4. Classical music isn't <u>my cup of tea.</u>

_____

5. Suzie was so excited, she <u>let the cat out of the bag.</u>

_____

© Evan-Moor Corp. • Daily Language Review • EMC 576

WEEK
33 **My Progress**

Name:

How many did you get correct each day? Color the squares.

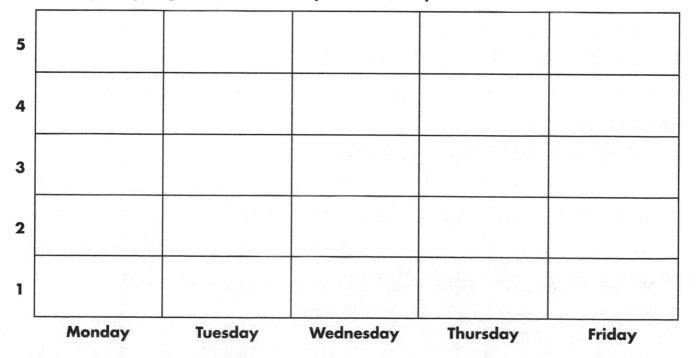

	Monday	Tuesday	Wednesday	Thursday	Friday
5					
4					
3					
2					
1					

© Evan-Moor Corp. • Daily Language Review • EMC 576

WEEK 34 Monday

Name: _____

© Evan-Moor Corp. • Daily Language Review • EMC 576

Correct these sentences.

1. charlie peter and tim we're late becuase they took there time

_____

2. they had to go to the principles office an appologize to there teacher

_____

Use context clues to determine the meaning of the bolded word.

3. Our teacher **enunciates** so that students who are learning English can understand her.

_____

Circle the correct way to divide this word into syllables.

4. ri di cu le   rid ic ule   rid i cule   ri dic ule

When might you hear the following?

5. "Look under N for number 35." _____

WEEK 34 Tuesday

Name: _____

© Evan-Moor Corp. • Daily Language Review • EMC 576

Write a fact about *straight hair*.

1. _____

If the guide words on a dictionary page are *collate* and *collision*, which words would be on the page?

2. collarbone   collector   collapse   collage   college

Correct these sentences.

3. sue played soccor and was a cheer leader but she always made time for homework

_____

4. because computers make finding facts easy they are a good source of infromation

_____

Does the underlined adverb tell how, when, where, or to what extent?

5. Kittens can be irritatingly playful. _____

Correct these sentences.

1. cuz ive never been back packing before i can't hardly weight to go

_____

2. I putted sew many things in my pack that it ways fourty pounds

_____

Write the abbreviation for *second*.

3. _____

Write the plural form of *mosquito*.

4. _____

Circle the words that are spelled correctly.

5. receive   ourselves   ownce   anoyc   boundary

Write a common noun for this proper noun.

1. Martin Luther King, Jr. Day _____

Write the comparative and superlative forms of *good*.

2. Comparative: _____   Superlative: _____

Correct these sentences.

3. greyhound bus drivers are reposnible for many passengers they must be alert

_____

4. mom has been buying soda hot dogs and buns she may have plans for sunday

_____

What is the following person's job?

5. Mr. Lee checked the screens in front of him and spoke into his headset, "You are cleared to land."

_____

Choose the best word to complete each sentence.

1. Mrs. Riley is patient with everyone in her class, so she deserves the _____ Award.
Procrastinator   Anxiety   Forbearance   Cantankerous

2. He was _____ when his science fair project collapsed as the judge looked at it.
chagrined   thrilled   fortunate   fulfilled

3. Frannie took her bow amid the applause and _____ of her fellow musicians.
disapproval   acclaim   scorn   alarm

4. The trail mix will provide _____ for the hike.
adornment   earnings   sustenance   bulk

5. She hopes to _____ her progress so that she can complete the course in half the time.
delay   furnish   dissolve   accelerate

Daily Language Review

WEEK 34 My Progress

Name:

How many did you get correct each day? Color the squares.

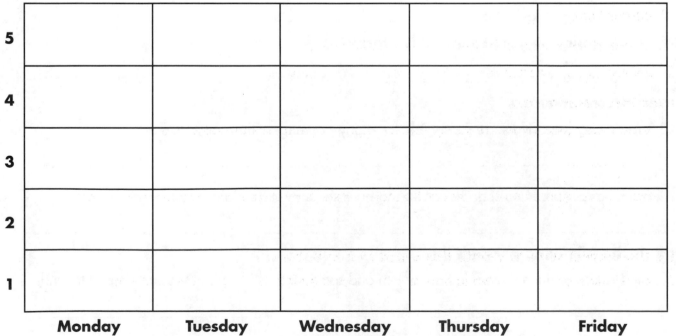

	Monday	Tuesday	Wednesday	Thursday	Friday
5					
4					
3					
2					
1					

WEEK 35 Monday

Name: _____

Correct these sentences.

1. impatient my lab partner ask when do you think youll compleat the project

    _____

2. i replyed ill be done as soon as i finish the research compose my ideas and print it out

    _____

Complete this analogy.

3. penguin : bird :: pizza : _____

Underline the complete subject of each sentence.

4. Thirty-two hungry, rowdy kindergartners burst through the lunchroom doors.

5. When she was asked to give her phone number, the new girl answered, "I haven't learned it."

Daily Language Review

WEEK 35 Tuesday

Name: _____

Does this word have a suffix, a prefix, both, or none?

1. extraordinary _____

Write a word that would belong in this category.

2. Denver   Sacramento   Austin   Louisville   _____

Correct these sentences.

3. on saturday june 5 ann will drive from arlington virginia to champaign illinois

    _____

4. tricias swiming imporved so much she moved from the novice to the intermmediate class

    _____

Circle the correct way to divide this word into syllables.

5. rev o lu tion ar y   re vo lu tion ar y   rev o lut ion ar y   re vol u tion ar y

WEEK 35 **Wednesday**

Name:

Correct these sentences.

1. how is sking and snowboreding different ask simons uncle

_____

2. tulips roses and lilacs line grannys pathway it smells like a flour shop

_____

Write the present form and the past participle of the verb _did._

3. Present form: _____   Past participle: _____

Circle the words that are not spelled correctly.

4. addresses   busineses   familys   countries   flies

Synonyms, antonyms, or homophones?

5. mature, develop   _____

WEEK 35 **Thursday**

Name:

Write the comparative and superlative adjectives of the word _beautiful._

1. Comparative: _____   Superlative: _____

Circle the adjectives in this sentence.

2. Aunt Carol's sixtieth birthday party was an exciting celebration of her many friends.

Correct these sentences.

3. somethings fishy exclaimmed the detective ill check it out

_____

4. I wish that I was tall like my friend john so then I could slamdunk the ball

_____

Explain what the underlined idiom in this sentence means.

5. I've been saving for rollerblades for over a year, but I finally see a light at the end of the tunnel.

_____

© Evan-Moor Corp. • Daily Language Review • EMC 576

WEEK 35 Friday

Name:

Label the subject or subjects and verb of each sentence.

1. This summer, my brother and I would like to learn to scuba dive.

   Subject(s): _____   Verb: _____

2. When I was mowing the lawn, a little frog hopped out of the grass.

   Subject(s): _____   Verb: _____

3. A sudden storm took the campers by surprise.

   Subject(s): _____   Verb: _____

4. I've never seen a purple cow.

   Subject(s): _____   Verb: _____

5. Misha's elderly aunt and her cat live down the street.

   Subject(s): _____   Verb: _____

WEEK 35 My Progress

Name:

How many did you get correct each day? Color the squares.

	Monday	Tuesday	Wednesday	Thursday	Friday
5					
4					
3					
2					
1					

WEEK 36 Monday Name:

Correct these sentences.

1. when water got hot it change in to water vaper this process is called evaporation

_____

2. when water vaper got cold it change in to a liqid this process is called condensation

_____

Are the underlined words a common noun or a proper noun?

3. My favorite treat is a <u>caramel apple</u> from the Chocolate Factory. _____

Metaphor or simile?

4. Mom has had her new washer repaired three times. She bought a lemon!

_____

Circle the word with the most syllables.

5. nourishment   humiliation   persevere   courageously

WEEK 36 Tuesday Name:

Circle the words that are spelled correctly.

1. awkward   allready   daughter   brought   althouh   stalke

Correct these sentences.

2. horton the elefant was determine when he said on birds egg and hatches it

_____

3. do you think dr seusss grinch wood like to eat green eggs and ham

_____

Interrogative or declarative?

4. Would you like me to check the tires? _____

5. The astronauts repaired the space station. _____

© Evan-Moor Corp. • Daily Language Review • EMC 576

WEEK 36 Wednesday

Name:

Correct these sentences.

1. I play the piccolo doug explained because its easyer to carrie a piccolo than a tuba

_____

2. after the movie jason ask do you think scientist will clon dna to create a living dinosaur

_____

Write a fact about *vegetables*.

3. _____

Synonyms, antonyms, or homophones?

4. grand, large _____

5. temporary, permanent _____

WEEK 36 Thursday

Name:

If the guide words on a dictionary page are *manicure* and *mantel*, which words would not be found on the page?

1. manmade   maniac   mannerism   mantilla   mantle

Rewrite this word, adding a suffix.

2. imagine _____

Correct these sentences.

3. must I take a water filter on the back packing trip ask bill I will carry water in my canteen

_____

4. you will be glad you did take the filter if you need more water the scout master answer

_____

Write an alliterative phrase about *dogs*.

5. _____

WEEK 36 Friday

Name: _____

Read the following paragraph and decide if the underlined parts have a capitalization error, a punctuation error, a spelling error, a noun/verb agreement error, or no error.

Solids, liquids and gases are all conducters of sound, but the speed of sound is different for each type
<u>   1   2   3</u>

of material. Sound waves travels much faster through solids and liquides than through gases.
              4   5

1. _____

2. _____

3. _____

4. _____

5. _____

WEEK 36 My Progress

Name: _____

How many did you get correct each day? Color the squares.

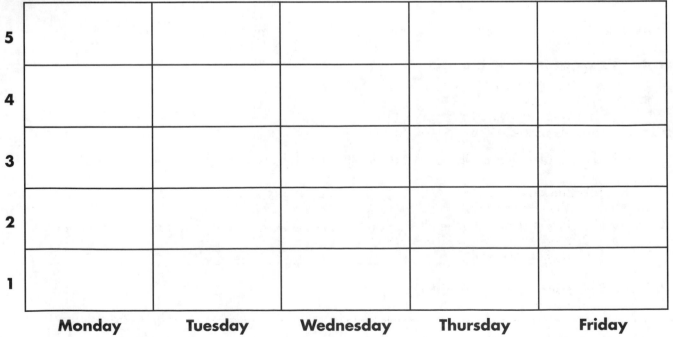

	Monday	Tuesday	Wednesday	Thursday	Friday
5					
4					
3					
2					
1					

Answer Key

WEEK 1

Monday
1. Does his cousin live in another city?
2. After James and Tim cleaned the garage, Grandma gave them five dollars.
3. plural
4. oxygen
5. umpire

Tuesday
1. Possible answer—construct
2. Possible answer—real
3. The children's valuables were stored in the teacher's closet.
4. That hot rod is the noisiest vehicle on my block.
5. interrogative

Wednesday
1. Wasn't there any milk in the refrigerator?
2. They're going to come to see me at 7 p.m.
3. heavy : light :: near : far
4. the airport
5. logic

Thursday
1. Ave.
2. lb.
3. dictionary
4. Let's play a game of soccer today.
5. Antonio was too big for his bike, so he sold it at Red Barn Flea Market.

Friday
1. tallest
2. heavier
3. hardest
4. busiest
5. longer

WEEK 2

Monday
1. My dad gave the present to Pete and me.
2. It wasn't a surprise; I knew he would do it.
3. arranged in the order in which something occurred
4. fact
5. opinion

Tuesday
1. Possible answer—won
2. fertilize
3. April is my favorite month of the year.
4. We made the last payment on our new computer.
5. They

Wednesday
1. The workmen laid a straight track for the freight train.
2. Maggie claimed she was too busy to do her homework.
3. closing
4. simile
5. gently

Thursday
1. shallot
2. 4
3. Mrs. Peters asked Mr. Beckman, "Will the concert start at 7:00 or 7:30?"
4. The workmen have come to fix the oven in Sammy's kitchen. OR The workman has come to fix the oven in Sammy's kitchen.
5. al

Friday
1. ist
2. less
3. ar
4. ly
5. ful

Monday

1. We had a flat tire, Amos was sunburned, and we got lost.
2. Chris thought, "I hope they will choose me for their team."
3. Dr.
4. Dear Dr. Ben Corliss: OR Dear Dr. Corliss:
5. an accomplishment to be proud of

Tuesday

1. antonyms
2. synonyms
3. "Look out below!" he called. "That rock is falling!"
4. Mother and her Polish friend, Mrs. Slovik, went to a Chinese restaurant.
5. gasoline

Wednesday

1. My friend, Mr. Murphy, visited churches in Canada, China, and Japan.
2. Their mom asked them to go to Black's Market for her.
3. circle—became lost; underline—had to be rescued
4. plural
5. taught

Thursday

1. won't
2. thesaurus
3. "Why do I have to do my homework now?" asked Tori.
4. "It's best to get your work done before you watch TV," said Mom.
5. Answers will vary—disappoint, reappoint

Friday

1. punctuation error (Ancient Egypt, a rich and prosperous nation,)
2. spelling error (grown)
3. capitalization error (Nile Valley)
4. punctuation error (raised cattle, geese, oxen, and pigs.)
5. no error

Monday

1. On April 2, Grandma Avery will celebrate her hundredth birthday.
2. I studied an interesting article, "Kayaking in Alaska," in <u>World</u> magazine.
3. grew
4. Answers will vary—Canada is a large country located north of the continental United States.
5. abandon

Tuesday

1. doesn't
2. The old, tired dog wants to lie down by the warm fire.
3. Are we supposed to read "The Plains" or "The Desert" in our books?
4. you would
5. Answers will vary—Sally was fourth in line as the dancers paraded back and forth across the stage.

Wednesday

1. The scariest story in *Horrifying Tales* was "Sounds" by T. S. Jones.
2. The farmer let them ride his horse.
3. graceful, rough, rocky, thick
4. Answers will vary—moan, own, phone, sewn, shone, stone, zone
5. receive

Thursday

1. myself
2. on an airplane
3. Dad sits in a chair to read his newspaper.
4. Is Miss Brown's English class going to recite Frost's poem?
5. adverb

Friday

Sentences may vary. Accept any reasonable sentence construction that contains all the information.

1. When the dog chased the cat, the cat ran up the tree.
2. Seline needed to buy a new dress because she was performing in a concert.
3. The team won the championship game because Tom and Seth hit home runs.
4. Would you like some lemonade to drink or some cookies to eat?
5. I'm so hungry, I think I could eat a horse.

WEEK 5

Monday

1. "Carl, will you help me do homework after school?"
2. "No, not today, because I'm going somewhere with my mom."
3. Scott's video game
4. They're
5. Go away; stop bothering me.

Tuesday

1. rep re sent a tive
2. how
3. Why doesn't he ever do his homework?
4. "It doesn't look like anything I've seen before," said Dr. Thomas.
5. circle—eruption; underline—lava oozed down the sides of the volcano, black smoke smothered the sunlight

Wednesday

1. After I'm done skating, I'll go to the library for an hour.
2. Did you get a letter from your pen pal?
3. adjective
4. antonyms
5. MI

Thursday

1. Past—dripped; Future—will drip
2. the elephant's tusks and ears
3. We stopped to use the bathroom, stretch and eat dinner.
4. Two boys' bikes were left in the center of Fifth Street on Friday, April 1.
5. declarative

Friday

1. zebra
2. jar
3. pitcher
4. string
5. hand

WEEK 6

Monday

1. Mrs. Lee has traveled to Europe, Asia, and South America.
2. I can't wait to travel by myself!
3. courage or strength of character
4. Possible answers—wrong, incorrect, erroneous, off-base.
5. nonfiction

Tuesday

1. what kind
2. twitch when I rub its back
3. Derek said he was too busy to make his bed.
4. Bob, Lee, and Al went to the Steinhart Aquarium to see the shark.
5. preveiw (preview)

Wednesday

1. Every Saturday, my brother watches *Iron Chef.*
2. Last summer, my friend Tara moved to Taos, New Mexico.
3. few
4. synonyms
5. homophones

Thursday

1. we're
2. Answers will vary—pretest, posttest, attest
3. "If we work hard," replied Judy, "we'll earn a good grade."
4. Michael asked, "How soon will breakfast be ready?"
5. past

Friday

1. well
2. Our
3. Who's
4. whose
5. are

Monday

1. That John Elway football belongs to my brother and me.
2. Michael and I ran in the Big Brothers' Marathon.
3. Possible sentence—They're standing over there, holding blue hats in their hands.
4. along
5. Answers will vary—talk, articulate, converse

Tuesday

1. Answers will vary—modern, contemporary
2. whistel (whistle)
3. Everyone was invited to their party.
4. Several butterflies and eagles flew overhead.
5. prefix

Wednesday

1. Those women's lunches all cost the same amount.
2. Jim likes apple, cherry, and peach pie, but I only like cake.
3. history

4. simile
5. preposition

Thursday

1. 4
2. 5
3. My sister tore off the book's cover.
4. Park City hired a coach for the boys' sports teams.
5. They

Friday

1. d
2. c
3. b
4. e
5. a

Monday

1. "Please tell me the answer to the riddle," begged Jose.
2. Will you help them paint their fence? OR Will you help those guys paint their fence?
3. yes
4. no
5. noun

Tuesday

1. carrot
2. Jeff sets his glasses on the table.
3. I need to write a thank-you note for the gift my aunt sent me.
4. something that draws one's attention to it
5. opinion

Wednesday

1. We read articles from <u>Newsweek</u>, <u>Time</u>, and <u>Cricket.</u>
2. While she poured tea, the girl spilled it on her mother's desk.
3. feline
4. siege
5. fierce, carefully planted, wheat

Thursday

1. closing
2. The words name different kinds of science.
3. While I waited for the griddle to get hot, I drew a design.
4. The sky opened up, and rain slammed to the ground!
5. mustn't

Friday

1. capitalization error (Kendo)
2. no error
3. spelling error (fragile)
4. punctuation error (Briefly lunging toward each other and then stepping back,)
5. no error

Monday
1. Who's that boy over there?
2. After the hen lays her eggs, she sits on them.
3. Any water form—stream, sea, bay
4. the books
5. ordinery (ordinary)

Tuesday
1. Possible sentence—The friendly puppy wagged its curly tail.
2. ob sti nate
3. oc cu pant
4. Pete and I got a new dog at Adam's Pet Shop.
5. Tim's shoes are too big, so he will buy a new pair at Ace Shoe Store.

Wednesday
1. The new desks in the classroom belong to Ana, Todd, and Kate.
2. Uncle Fred bought us pizza at Freddie's.
3. object pronoun
4. mouse
5. When Susan got out of bed, she looked out her window to check the weather.

Thursday
1. Rd.
2. receiving, worrying, planning
3. Tom worries constantly about his end-of-the-year project.
4. The thirsty boy drank the Dr. Pepper in one swallow.
5. synonyms

Friday
Topic sentence: Sentence 8
Main idea: How seeds travel
Supporting details: Sentences 1, 4, 5, and 6

Monday
1. Native Americans believed that spirits protected them.
2. There were hundreds of tribes in America when Christopher Columbus landed.
3. fact
4. higher
5. lowest

Tuesday
1. Opinions will vary—Eliminating pollution is everyone's job.
2. peppermint
3. I have the addresses of friends living in other countries.
4. Mrs. Moore's business is taking pictures of family groups.
5. Possible sentence—I picked four strawberries for the cobbler.

Wednesday
1. The climate along the equator is different from the climate in Alaska.
2. His vehicle had a punctured tire, so he waited by the side of the road.
3. catch
4. imperative
5. purchases

Thursday
1. shuttle
2. foxes, wolves
3. Mr. Tuttle asked, "Did you study for your math test?"
4. I spent a day at the library writing my essay for English.
5. has lasted a long time, despite our differences

Friday
1. be just the perfect thing
2. in good health
3. find out the real cause
4. is involved in many matters
5. Face reality.

Monday

1. The words impolite and inconsiderate are close in meaning.
2. Dr. Landry's motto is "Always be prepared."
3. Possible answers—stranger, strangely, strangest
4. simile
5. Possible answers—quiet, lull, settle

Tuesday

1. cruel, school, cool, rule
2. chute, newt, route, suit
3. "Well, do you think you can help me on Saturday?"
4. "I can help you Monday, Jay, if that's not too late."
5. Sentences will vary—Whirling wheels whizzed by me.

Wednesday

1. All the ice in the lemonade began to disappear.
2. The jelly in Slim's sandwich dripped out onto his shirt.
3. technology, substituted
4. circle—ticket line was so long; underline—missed the first part of the movie
5. man, city

Thursday

1. Comparative—heavier; Superlative—heaviest
2. synonyms
3. We catch that bus at the corner of Elm Street and First Avenue.
4. Traveler Airlines allows you to take one suitcase and a carry-on bag.
5. scent

Friday

1. ful
2. ment
3. less
4. ly
5. ar, or

Monday

1. The paddleboats moved along the Missouri River.
2. "Land ahoy!" the first mate shouted.
3. implied
4. temperature
5. armored, mossy, dark

Tuesday

1. prepositional phrase
2. We won't have an assignment until Wednesday, September 3.
3. There were three pieces of pizza on the plate. Kelly took the largest one.
4. to, with
5. Possible answers—track, pursue, hunt

Wednesday

1. Six geese were searching for some delicious worms to eat.
2. Last year, we spent our vacation at Uncle Jim's farm.
3. loose board
4. Who's
5. overhead

Thursday

1. fact
2. common noun
3. The hailstones pounded the roofs during the storm.
4. Dr. Rivers stood beside his patient's bed and said, "Say ahhhh."
5. polite

Friday

1. not a sentence
2. sentence
   circle—machine
   underline—responded to his command
3. not a sentence
4. sentence
   circle—Tom, Franco, Seline, and Julie
   underline—played
5. sentence
   circle—He
   underline—lurched and stumbled against the table

Monday

1. Weren't there any cookies left?
2. "Hello out there!" Terry's voice was muffled by his mask.
3. into
4. well
5. stan dard ize

Tuesday

1. authentic
2. subject
3. Why can't he ever get here on time?
4. The singers will end the show with their version of "It's a Small World."
5. fact

Wednesday

1. The Sioux lived on the Great Plains and tracked buffalo.
2. Woodland tribes, like the Onondaga, made their homes of wood.
3. yard
4. distruction (destruction)
5. They

Thursday

1. they're
2. almanac OR encyclopedia
3. Who's going to collect the six o'clock mail when it's delivered?
4. I've no idea what you're talking about.
5. Answers will vary—mean, hurtful, fierce

Friday

1. capitalization error (Olympic Games)
2. punctuation error (Olympus, Greece,)
3. punctuation error (Today's)
4. spelling error (Approximately)
5. no error

Monday

1. My favorite candies are made out of Swiss chocolate.
2. Boris's baby sister tore the library book pages.
3. condense (dense)
4. worthless
5. The stunt diver

Tuesday

1. radii
2. an, a
3. The dog's owners wrote a poem about their pet.
4. Can you play quietly until the meeting is adjourned?
5. Comparative—handsomer; Superlative—handsomest

Wednesday

1. H. W. Longfellow wrote, "Listen, my children, and you shall hear of the midnight ride of Paul Revere."
2. The weathercaster told the temperature, explained the fog, and gave a forecast.
3. give help in a crisis
4. bound
5. wept

Thursday

1. subject pronoun
2. adverb
3. I will lay the photograph on that table in plain view.
4. Flowers of every color bloomed in Professor Shaw's garden.
5. keep something secret

Friday

Sentences may vary. Accept any reasonable sentence construction that contains all the information.

1. Carrying their helmets in their hands, the football team ran onto the field.
2. Pam used the library browser to find a book for her report, and then she checked out the book.
3. When Tom fell off the bike, he learned that racing bikes can be dangerous.
4. Ahmad became our new student body president when he got the most votes in the election.
5. Since Ashley lives next door to me, she feeds my puppies when I'm gone.
   OR Ashley, who lives next door to me, feeds my puppies when I'm gone.

Monday

1. Do you think Mr. Long will accept my report if it's handwritten?
2. My granddad believes you should always carry a handkerchief.
3. for
4. metaphor
5. numerel, vowal (numeral, vowel)

Tuesday

1. beanbag
2. Blvd.
3. If I were a doctor, I would help people stay well.
4. County Hospital is located on the corner of King Way and State Street.
5. present

Wednesday

1. My brother's best riddle is, "What kind of house weighs the least?"
2. The answer is, "A lighthouse."
3. They all are two-dimensional shapes.
4. hydrangea, hunger
5. where

Thursday

1. prefix
2. half
3. Mrs. Turlock says that I must learn how to use parentheses.
4. I can't imagine a more ridiculous idea!
5. antonyms

Friday

1. Subject–She;
   Verb–crept
2. Subject–She;
   Verbs–loved, walk
3. Subject–Toby;
   Verb–gave
4. Subject–I;
   Verbs–would like, leave
5. Subject–girls;
   Verbs–smiled, clapped

Monday

1. "Scott, make your arms slice into the water!" shouted Coach Storm.
2. He reminded him, "Keep your kick going strong out of your turns."
3. circle—I missed the previous class; underline—I didn't understand the questions on the test.
4. To Whom It May Concern:
5. Sentences will vary—The carpenter who will build the garage has already billed my parents for the plans.

Tuesday

1. feel, felon, fence
2. "I already finished doing the dishes," Mom sighed.
3. "Please," she said, "put your dirty plate on the drainboard before you leave."
4. effect
5. sandboxes

Wednesday

1. The waitress said, "Today we have strawberries, raspberries, and blackberries."
2. "Would you like some whipped cream with your berries?" she asked.
3. imperative, exclamatory
4. subject pronoun
5. entertain, envision, envelope

Thursday

1. atlas
2. real
3. The baby looks like she's going to bawl.
4. The baby sitter asked, "Do you have any ideas about what we should do?"
5. verb

Friday

1. am, was, been
2. come, came, come
3. do, did, done
4. eat, ate, eaten
5. see, saw, seen

Monday
1. At midnight, we heard Jim's friends searching for snacks in the cupboard.
2. How many cartons came in the mail shipment this afternoon?
3. predicate
4. 5430 Broad Ave. #310
   Oakland, CA 94618
5. Opinions will vary—It is important to protect the natural environments of endangered species.

Tuesday
1. there have
2. synonyms
3. Whose dog is that one over there? OR Whose dogs are those over there?
4. I wish I could stay at home to meet you, but I have to go.
5. for a long visit

Wednesday
1. Nurse Nancy gave her a clean bandage for her knee.
2. It may not seem right, but it's always been the rule.
3. scale
4. hung

5. Sentences will vary—I would like to have a sled made out of wood.

Thursday
1. atmophere (atmosphere)
2. common noun
3. proper noun
4. I can't wait to try the snacks: Nicole made cake, Sara made candy, and Bob made pie. OR I can't wait to try the snacks. Nicole made cake, Sara made candy, and Bob made pie.
5. Farmer Ted dug a hole in his garden for a compost pit.

Friday
1. presidents—Add **s** to the end of most words.
2. benches—If a word ends in **ch**, add **es**.
3. varieties—If a word ends in a consonant followed by **y**, change the **y** to **i** and add **es**.
4. journeys—If the word ends in a vowel followed by **y**, just add **s**.
5. lives—Some words ending in **fe** are formed by changing the **f** to **v** and adding **es**.

Monday
1. Sasha whispered to herself, "Where did John hide mom's ring?"
2. I read two chapters of *Tom Sawyer* every night before I go to bed.
3. not being aware or not paying attention
4. Where, wear
5. rinsing

Tuesday
1. o'clock
2. Sentences will vary—There were two bridal attendants in attendance at the shower.
3. The dishes on the shelves fell during the earthquake.
4. "The mountain in the painting is Mt. Hood," said the museum guide.
5. inside address

Wednesday
1. Mrs. Springs dries flowers for bouquets.
2. The park across the street from my house is called Central Park.
3. object pronoun

4. opinion
5. what kind

Thursday
1. common noun
2. interrogative
3. Aunt Jo had to fly to Denver on her way to St. Louis.
4. Put extra writing paper, scissors, pencils, and glue in the tub.
5. antonyms

Friday
1. spelling error (spotted)
2. no error
3. capitalization error (the)
4. capitalization error (million)
5. punctuation error (lives in caves, under rocks and logs,)

Monday

1. No one in the family had ever been to Hawaii.
2. "How many boxes of cookies did you sell?" the troop leader asked.
3. how
4. fewer
5. li a bil i ty

Tuesday

1. peaceful
2. geranium
3. To me, New Year's Day means Grandma's chili and a family feast.
4. The principal said, "Make sure your children have a quiet time for homework." OR The principal said, "Make sure your child has a quiet time for homework."
5. declarative

Wednesday

1. "The cup should be level when you pour the punch," warned Mom.
2. "I can't believe I won the jackpot!" Carlos screamed.
3. fought
4. singular possessive
5. plural possessive

Thursday

1. remember
2. midnight, midway, midsummer, midyear
3. Scott came home at 8:30 after the Boy Scout meeting.
4. His friends asked Mrs. Morrow to come to his recital.
5. the post office or shipping center

Friday

Sentences will vary but should include all the information.

1. My friends and I like to go to the gym and work out three times a week.
2. My coach, Mr. Sutter, believes that practice is the key to winning.
3. This morning, the bushes wore new coats of white because there was a snowstorm last night.
4. At first when I talked with my grandma on the phone, she sounded weak and shaky, but by the time we hung up, her voice was full of life.
5. Mowing the lawn is a big job because, besides cutting the grass, you have to service the mower and edge the sidewalk.

Monday

1. has'nt (hasn't)
2. "On Friday, my friends and I will go to Central Zoo," said Sue.
3. "Peter, would you rather see the tiger, the lion, or the chimp?"
4. verb—The words show action.
5. tomatoes

Tuesday

1. metaphor
2. insted (instead)
3. Their wedding cake was so tall, it almost reached the ceiling.
4. The bride's veil, borrowed from her aunt, looked like a shiny cloud.
5. more than enough

Wednesday

1. In my room, I've displayed my collection of caps from every baseball team.
2. It's fun to wear one and imagine yourself at bat, facing Randy Johnson.
3. telephone book
4. miscellaneous
5. circle—his son was too young; underline—his wife Hatshepsut became pharaoh

Thursday

1. dissolute
2. peace
3. My uncle won the Distinguished Flying Cross for his bravery.
4. We're all very proud of his special distinction.
5. there, softly

Friday

1. got angry
2. was afraid, perform
3. go another time
4. very inexpensively
5. putting herself in danger

Monday
1. "Can you come over to watch *Jeopardy*?" asked Jamal.
2. "My mom is out of town, so I'll have to ask Grandpa," Travis answered.
3. circle—some great disaster struck; underline—smoke stains on the walls, scattered vessels
4. grown
5. thorough, incomplete

Tuesday
1. swept
2. couch, allow, house, trout, bough
3. Teresa will pick up the papers, sweep, and dust.
4. "What do you want to be responsible for?" asked Mrs. Timms.
5. fact

Wednesday
1. All of the players chose Mr. Rupp as the best basketball coach. OR All of them chose Mr. Rupp as the best basketball coach.
2. Have you ever heard the Beatles' song "Yellow Submarine"?
3. speak
4. string, struggle, strident
5. basket

Thursday
1. puzzle
2. a football or soccer game
3. Sydney asked, "Will we see sharks at Ocean World?"
4. After school, I saw Peter, who asked, "Can you stop by my house?"
5. diction

Friday
1. was
2. do
3. him
4. sheep
5. Who's

Monday
1. Josh, Tori, and Maddie went to Disney World.
2. They rode Space Mountain, Rock 'n' Roller Coaster, and Test Track.
3. think about for a long time
4. manufacture, civilization
5. plural possessive

Tuesday
1. mouth-watering, Mother's, hungry
2. guise
3. If you join the book club, you will receive a subscription to *Highlights*.
4. Perk's Supreme is the only coffee that my mother likes.
5. After the service, of his relatives, to the restaurant

Wednesday
1. "If we go to study hall now," Dave boasted, "we'll be finished first."
2. Huck Finn is a fictional character created by Mark Twain.
3. Sept.
4. Possible answers—statement, stately, stateside
5. you

Thursday
1. Possible synonyms—precise, right, correct; possible antonyms—inaccurate, incorrect, wrong
2. Possible synonyms—attractive, gorgeous, stunning, stylish; possible antonyms—plain, unattractive, frumpy
3. Meeker's Student Council voted to visit hospitals on Thanksgiving.
4. The teachers will go to Ralph's to buy the food.
5. mos qui to

Friday
1. Subject—puppy; Verbs—wagged, barked
2. Subject—Slippery Rock; Verb—is
3. Subject—squirrel; Verbs—gathered, stored
4. Subject—you; Verbs—did, do
5. Subject—vacation; Verb—is

Monday

1. Keli and Glen want to go horseback riding on Friday at 3 o'clock.
2. The Smith twins, Sara and Emily, wear matching outfits.
3. Accept any "falling" sound—kerplop, thump
4. future
5. body

Tuesday

1. lie
2. clasp, clarinet, clam
3. When I'm tired of writing, I stand up and breathe deeply.
4. often what I think I keyboard is not what's on the page.
5. synonyms

Wednesday

1. When I asked, "Who is it?" I heard a voice reply, "It's only me." (Although *me* is incorrect, it can be used in a quotation. Use this as an authentic moment to discuss *It is I.*)
2. Humpty Dumpty posed an impossible challenge for the king's men.
3. Answers will vary—The amount of homework assigned nightly varies.
4. locate/discover, original/first
5. to what extent

Thursday

1. Arturo's
2. absolutely necessary
3. "It's almost lunchtime!" shouted Simon.
4. Hurry! Let's go to Carpenter Beach for a picnic!
5. which ones

Friday

1. no error
2. punctuation error (came from?)
3. capitalization error (Italy)
4. spelling error (dessert)
5. spelling error (popularizing)

Monday

1. Of all the stars in the sky, the sun is the closest to Earth.
2. It's a ball of burning gases that's about five billion years old.
3. where or how
4. metaphor
5. singular

Tuesday

1. object pronoun
2. Do you think that someday someone will travel all the way to Mars?
3. Sid knows that the letter was supposed to have arrived on June 10 by 10 a.m.
4. is always reading
5. toddler

Wednesday

1. You'd better clean up that mess quickly!
2. Boris and Jean packed the pictures for the Air Express truck.
3. too
4. not a sentence
5. sentence

Thursday

1. we'll
2. adverb
3. In his poem "Primer Lesson," Carl Sandburg wrote, "Look out how you use proud words."
4. Isn't it almost time for the assembly?
5. synonyms

Friday

Sentences will vary. Accept any reasonable sentence construction that contains all the information.

1. Marilyn tried on hiking boots, walking shoes, and ballet slippers before she bought some sandals.
2. We drove to the camping store to buy a tent cover, but when we got there the store was closed.
3. The car slid off the road when it turned the corner because the road was covered with black ice.
4. Jo went to visit her only sister, who lives in St. Louis.
5. I couldn't make cookies because the carton of eggs in the refrigerator had only one egg in it.

Monday

1. These sentences are beginning to all look alike.
2. "Honey is a treat for bears," said the zookeeper.
3. the teachers' books
4. Sentences will vary—She carried her plain black suitcase onto the plane.
5. fact

Tuesday

1. Comparative—quieter; Superlative—quietest
2. kindergartners, ball, bees, hive
3. I use Post-it® notes to label the pages that need corrections.
4. After ten laps around the track, his chest heaves in and out as he breathes.
5. en ve lope

Wednesday

1. My gardener suggests I plant tulips, lilacs, and a rose.
2. Have you had to have your teeth pulled by a dentist?

3. few
4. suffix
5. prefix

Thursday

1. circle—extreme daytime heat; underline—drove across the desert at night
2. thesaurus
3. I bought kiwi from Mexico and pineapple from Hawaii.
4. "Can you get some peaches for me?" asked Frank.
5. March 13, 1982,

Friday

1. get straight to the basic facts of the matter
2. enjoys
3. talking nonsense
4. like someone who doesn't fit in
5. failed miserably

Monday

1. Ray will pick up his new pickup at Truck City tomorrow.
2. During the last rainstorm, my roof sprang a leak.
3. an unusual ability to influence people and inspire devotion
4. greeting
5. in her highchair

Tuesday

1. qt.
2. Answers will vary—Greeley
3. Answers will vary—Sun Land Company
4. The Scott Boys' Bike Club meets on Wednesday after school.
5. Would you like to come to the next meeting as my guest?

Wednesday

1. When beavers build dams, every member of a beaver family helps.
2. Mother, Father, and three or four younger beavers work together.
3. Comparative—easier; Superlative—easiest

4. lock
5. the transparent plastic crate

Thursday

1. They
2. it
3. There are many different kinds of lettuce, like romaine and bibb.
4. Chef Dennis uses four lettuces in his famous Harvest Salad.
5. circle—Don watched a DVD; underline—when Dad turned on the computer, the battery was low.

Friday

1. lost
2. showed
3. they're
4. eat
5. sung

Monday

1. I named my pet George because I got him at George's Pet Store.
2. When I pet George, I say, "You're my best friend."
3. subject pronoun
4. object pronoun
5. Answers will vary—They are all skills or hobbies that use yarn or thread to make things.

Tuesday

1. verb
2. adjective
3. The Navajo people are famous for their beautiful rugs.
4. Historically, they lived on the Southwestern Plains.
5. homophones

Wednesday

1. Pete found his favorite DVD, "Transformers," under his bed.
2. Dr. Morgan X-rayed Annie's teeth and said, "No cavities!" (Accept a period or an exclamation point.)
3. Answers will vary—autograph, telegraph, paragraph, homograph
4. in math class
5. stoop, stone

Thursday

1. people
2. The traffic wasn't bad this morning. Maybe it's a holiday. OR The traffic wasn't bad this morning, so maybe it's a holiday.
3. Frank complained, "My hands are chapped because of the cold, wet weather."
4. Past—forbade; Future—will forbid
5. The enormous elephants, two fierce tigers, a gawky llama, and Bobo the trained bear

Friday

1. whole, hole
2. write, right
3. principal, principle
4. rays, raise, raze
5. stationery, stationary

Monday

1. Heather wove a small blanket for the baby's bed.
2. Drew knew the right answer before the teacher had asked the question.
3. holding one's interest completely
4. construct
5. port

Tuesday

1. lu mi nous
2. The lady waved her hand at her realtor and said, "We want that house."
3. The house was designed by a famous architect named Frank Lloyd Wright.
4. subject
5. a suffix

Wednesday

1. Mr. Gerk announced, "If I don't have coffee, my day is off to a bad start."
2. "Here, sir," said Hillary, "I think I can help," as she held out a steaming mug.
3. opinion
4. chocolates, rhythms
5. suddenly, regrettably, soon

Thursday

1. what kind
2. which ones
3. "Run six laps before coming to class," Coach O'Keefe said.
4. Thirty-two different species of birds live near Lake Oswego.
5. metaphor

Friday

1. spelling error (scared)
2. no error
3. capitalization error (Amazon Rainforest)
4. punctuation error (deserted, unpaved)
5. no error

Daily Language Review • EMC 576 • © Evan-Moor Corp.

WEEK 29

Monday
1. Molly and Max, his two terriers, make life exciting at Josh's house.
2. We read the Declaration of Independence in our class.
3. Comparative—worse; Superlative—worst
4. no
5. yes

Tuesday
1. circle—Japanese Beetle larvae were found in a backyard garden; underline—Forest Service officials are combing the area
2. Stuart Little is a caring newcomer to the Little family.
3. Nashville, Tennessee, is the capital of that state.
4. leased
5. least

Wednesday
1. "A trip to the Museum of Natural History is a treat!" exclaimed Sara.
2. "Tomorrow" is my favorite song from <u>Annie.</u>

3. closing
4. in this helter-skelter world, of my own
5. bone

Thursday
1. D.C.
2. imperative
3. Imagine an arbor with roses cascading from its branches.
4. My garden is like a vegetable stand with daily produce specials.
5. heav i er

Friday
1. Subjects—Pat, Mike; Verb—went
2. Subject—Mike; Verb—brought
3. Subject—Pat; Verb—caught
4. Subject—fish; Verb—was
5. Subject—he; Verb—threw

WEEK 30

Monday
1. Jose found a wallet with receipts from an account at World Bank.
2. When he returned the wallet to Security, he received a reward of $50.
3. weighed down or burdened
4. present
5. past

Tuesday
1. opinion
2. pessimistic
3. Dr. Lee is a pediatrician who is like a grandfather to his patients.
4. Why didn't Julie take driver's education this summer?
5. Sentences will vary—I sent a card to my grandma that had a rose scent to it.

Wednesday
1. Mr. Smith, the art teacher, lent me the book about Picasso.
2. Peter and I want to try to paint a mural in Picasso's style.
3. verb

4. happen
5. what kind

Thursday
1. future
2. past
3. "Noises, especially loud ones, are frightening at night," explained Fred.
4. My kitten, Ollie, naps, wakes up and stretches, and then sleeps some more.
5. Comparative—funnier; Superlative—funniest

Friday
1. c
2. d
3. e
4. b
5. a

Monday
1. The Pioneer Society is a group of descendants of families that homesteaded in the West.
2. My great-grandmother's parents were part of that original settlement.
3. Answers will vary—bring, fetch, return
4. Answers will vary—remote, distant, isolated
5. where

Tuesday
1. study carefully
2. How many of us are there?
3. Sal, Ron, and I went out to our new clubhouse.
4. They are different kinds of pasta.
5. They are things a baby uses.

Wednesday
1. My little cousin always says, "Give me five!"
2. The phone rang just as Mom was leaving the house.
3. circle—late takeoff in Los Angeles; underline—missed connection in Denver
4. Opinions will vary—Television shows contain too much violence.
5. presentible (presentable)

Thursday
1. computer technician
2. very important or necessary
3. I just finished reading a book entitled Through My Eyes by Ruby Bridges.

4. It described her experience as the only black student in her school.
5. dove into the water and swam to victory

Friday
1. spelling error (comprehension)
2. spelling error (strategies)
3. punctuation error (that you use?)
4. punctuation error (As you read,)
5. punctuation error (After you read,)

Monday
1. Pebbles and Bam Bam are characters in the movie The Flintstones.
2. Because it snowed, Mr. Ruiz, the building manager, cleared the walks.
3. simile
4. natcheral (natural)
5. 1 a.m.

Tuesday
1. band members' uniforms
2. Homer Spit is a piece of land that juts into Kamishak Bay from Alaska.
3. The Empress Hotel in Victoria, British Columbia, has a lovely dining room.
4. homophones
5. 1—breadwinner; 2—breakage; 3—breakfast; 4—breeze; 5—brevity

Wednesday
1. My brothers and I like to play Monopoly® on Saturday afternoons.
2. Eating an apple every day is supposed to keep the doctor away.
3. would have
4. verb
5. plywood

Thursday
1. Sentences will vary—She changed the horse's gait as they rode through the gate.
2. dab, damask
3. Once upon a time, there were a king, a queen, and a magnificent castle.

4. Please put up your umbrella after you're outside the door.
5. embankment

Friday
Answers will vary, but they should be capitalized and punctuated correctly.

Monday
1. I use chocolate bars, marshmallows, and crackers to make a tasty dessert.
2. The name of the dessert's s'mores, and you will want more after your first one.
3. standard
4. conspire
5. with a grain of salt

Tuesday
1. did snore last night
2. overly proud of one's looks, abilities, or accomplishments
3. "I believe that Goldilocks was a trespasser!" announced the teacher.
4. "I agree with your assessment," replied the student.

5. Answers will vary—microscope, telescope, periscope

Wednesday
1. Black widow spiders and Mexican tarantulas are fearsome insects.
2. Sometimes I wish I were an eagle soaring through the clear blue sky.
3. Answer must be something the lion hunts—zebra
4. verb
5. preposition

Thursday
1. them
2. square
3. Tonya said, "My legs go to sleep when I sit on them."

4. Stephen said, "Oh, my legs go to sleep when I'm lying on the bed."
5. adverb

Friday
1. extremely jealous
2. far superior
3. a sure thing
4. something I don't like
5. gave away the secret

WEEK 34

Monday
1. Charlie, Peter, and Tim were late because they took their time.
2. They had to go to the principal's office and apologize to their teacher.
3. Pronounces words, especially in a clear voice
4. rid i cule
5. when you are playing bingo

Tuesday
1. Facts will vary—Some people have straight hair, and some people have curly hair.
2. collector, college
3. Sue played soccer and was a cheerleader, but she always made time for homework.

4. Because computers make finding facts easy, they are a good source of information.
5. to what extent

Wednesday
1. Because I've never been backpacking before, I can hardly wait to go.
2. I put so many things in my pack that it weighs forty pounds.
3. sec.
4. mosquitoes
5. receive, ourselves, boundary

Thursday
1. holiday
2. Comparative—better; Superlative—best

3. Greyhound bus drivers are responsible for many passengers, so they must be alert.
4. Mom has been buying soda, hot dogs, and buns. She may have plans for Sunday.
5. air traffic controller

Friday
1. Forbearance
2. chagrined
3. acclaim
4. sustenance
5. accelerate

WEEK 35

Monday
1. Impatiently, my lab partner asked, "When do you think you'll complete the project?"
2. I replied, "It'll be done as soon as I finish the research, compose my ideas, and print it out."
3. food
4. thirty-two hungry, rowdy kindergartners
5. the new girl

Tuesday
1. both
2. any state capital
3. On Saturday, June 5, Ann will drive from Arlington, Virginia, to Champaign, Illinois.

4. Tricia's swimming improved so much, she moved from the novice to the intermediate class.
5. rev o lu tion ar y

Wednesday
1. "How are skiing and snowboarding different?" asked Simon's uncle.
2. Tulips, roses, and lilacs line Granny's pathway. It smells like a flower shop.
3. Present form—do; Past participle—done
4. businesses, familys (businesses, families)
5. synonyms

Thursday
1. Comparative—more beautiful; Superlative—most beautiful

2. Aunt Carol's, sixtieth, birthday, exciting, her, many
3. "Something's fishy!" exclaimed the detective. "I'll check it out!"
4. I wish that I were tall like my friend John, so then I could slam-dunk the ball.
5. A long-searched-for goal is within reach.

Friday
1. Subjects—My brother, I; Verb—would like
2. Subject—frog; Verb—hopped
3. Subject—storm; Verb—took
4. Subject—I; Verb—have seen
5. Subjects—aunt, cat; Verb—live

WEEK 36

Monday
1. When water gets hot, it changes into water vapor. This process is called evaporation.
2. When water vapor gets cold, it changes into a liquid. This process is called condensation.
3. common noun
4. metaphor
5. humiliation

Tuesday
1. awkward, daughter, brought
2. Horton the Elephant was determined when he sat on the bird's egg and hatched it.
3. Do you think Dr. Seuss's Grinch would like to eat green eggs and ham?
4. interrogative
5. declarative

Wednesday
1. "I play the piccolo," Doug explained, "because it's easier to carry a piccolo than a tuba."
2. After the movie, Jason asked, "Do you think scientists will clone DNA to create a living dinosaur?"
3. Facts will vary—Some vegetables are root vegetables, and some are leaf vegetables.
4. synonyms
5. antonyms

Thursday
1. maniac, mantilla, mantle
2. Answers will vary—imagination, imaginary
3. "Must I take a water filter on the backpacking trip?" asked Bill. "I will carry water in my canteen."

4. "You will be glad you did take the filter if you need more water," the scoutmaster answered.
5. Sentences will vary. All or nearly all words must begin with the same sound—Davy's dogs dig dutifully.

Friday
1. punctuation error (solids, liquids, and gases)
2. spelling error (conductors)
3. no error
4. noun/verb agreement error (Sound waves travel)
5. spelling error (liquids)

Language GRADE 6+
Fundamentals

Free Sampler

What?

Evan-Moor's *Language Fundamentals* is your one-stop resource for reteaching and additional practice of grammar, mechanics, and usage.

- 160 student-friendly activity pages, scaffolded to accommodate students' varied skill levels

- Multiple-choice review pages for assessment and standardized test preparation

- Paragraph Editing pages that provide "real-world" application of skills

Why?

- You use *Daily Language Review*, but some students need further skill reinforcement. *Language Fundamentals* is just what you need.

- Once you've identified the skills the student has not mastered, use pages from *Language Fundamentals* for targeted practice.

The six pages that follow give you a sample of the variety and scope of practice found in *Language Fundamentals*, Grade 6+.

Table of Contents

> Some pronouns do not name the word they replace.
> These are called indefinite pronouns.
>
> | | | | | |
> |---|---|---|---|---|
> | all | another | anybody | anyone | anything |
> | both | each | everybody | everyone | everything |
> | few | many | most | none | no one |
> | nothing | one | other | several | some |
> | somebody | something | such | | |
>
> **Most** are coming to graduation.
> **Nothing** was done correctly.
> **Somebody** needs to do **something.**

Circle the correct indefinite pronoun to complete the sentence.

1. We need _____ to help out this weekend for the class cleanup.
   (one, everybody, all)

2. _____ have signed up for litter patrol in the park.
   (Each, Several, Other)

3. Surprisingly, _____ has volunteered yet to work at the beach.
   (few, another, no one)

4. _____ needs to pick up the trash there.
   (Somebody, Both, Most)

5. _____ leave behind bottles and cans.
   (Both, None, Many)

6. Can _____ explain why caring for the environment is so important?
   (some, anyone, something)

7. Actually, _____ have through their actions and attitudes.
   (none, such, many)

8. For example, just about _____ recycles today.
   (everyone, everything, most)

> Some pronouns are used to ask a question.
> These are called interrogative pronouns.
>
> **what   who   which   whose   whom**
>
> **What** happened to our luggage?
> **Who** is going to find our suitcase?
> **Which** color suitcase is yours?
> **Whose** bag is missing?
> With **whom** should we discuss the lost bag?

Complete each sentence with the correct interrogative pronoun from the box above. Write the word on the line.

1. _____ is organizing the surprise party?

2. _____ can I do to help?

3. _____ idea was it to go ice skating?

4. _____ if they don't like to ice-skate?

5. _____ place did you tell them?

6. _____ said that park had an ice-skating rink?

7. To _____ did you give that information?

8. _____ kids should we call first?

9. _____ will we do if everyone shows up at the wrong place?

10. _____ surprise is likely to be greater, theirs or ours, if the plan works?

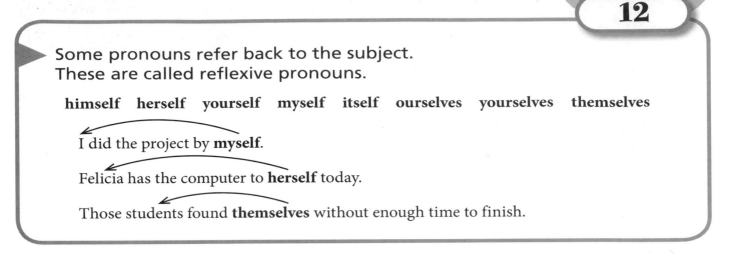

Some pronouns refer back to the subject.
These are called reflexive pronouns.

himself   herself   yourself   myself   itself   ourselves   yourselves   themselves

I did the project by **myself**.

Felicia has the computer to **herself** today.

Those students found **themselves** without enough time to finish.

Read each sentence. Underline the subject, then circle the correct reflexive pronoun to complete the sentence.

1. You need the kitchen to _____ because you are a messy cook.
   (itself, yourself)

2. Dad and Mom want the porch to _____ while they discuss our family vacation.
   (themselves, ourselves)

3. Hunter has planned a great trip for us all by _____.
   (himself, ourselves)

4. Emily says she will help you in the kitchen or clean up by _____.
   (yourself, herself)

5. Too bad that pan cannot clean _____!
   (itself, myself)

6. We are bringing a lot of great food for _____ to the beach house.
   (ourselves, yourselves)

   Sample pages from Language Fundamentals • EMC 2756 • © Evan-Moor Corp.

Name _____

Fill in the bubble next to the correct answer.

1. Identify the correct interrogative pronoun to complete the sentence.
   With _____ will you attend the dance?
   (A) what
   (B) whom
   (C) whose
   (D) which

2. Choose the correct reflexive pronoun to complete the sentence.
   Jenny and Dan want to see the project for _____.
   (A) theirselves
   (B) ourselves
   (C) themselves
   (D) themself

3. Complete the sentence with the correct indefinite pronoun.
   _____ is needed in that play to make it more fun to watch.
   (A) Few
   (B) None
   (C) Both
   (D) Something

4. Identify the correct interrogative pronoun to complete the sentence.
   _____ has to come the farthest to camp?
   (A) Who
   (B) Whom
   (C) Which
   (D) Whose

5. Choose the correct reflexive pronoun to complete the sentence.
   Gavin and Michael want to put the team together _____.
   (A) himself
   (B) themselves
   (C) theirselves
   (D) itself

Proofread these paragraphs. Find the 10 errors, cross them out, and write the words correctly above them.

On a sunny summer day, many neighbors visit our backyard. Most yards in the neighborhood are small, but our is large. My friends and me have room for running and shady spots for resting. Last night, my dad and mom cooked hot dogs on the grill in the backyard. Some parents don't cook outside, but my like to cook for a crowd in our backyard.

Almost all of the neighbors came over. Ms. Lee brought potato salad. I like potato salad, and her's is the best I've ever tasted. Mr. Carson brought lemonade and soda. Him and Ms. Carson brought lawn chairs, too. There lawn chairs provided all of us places to sit while we waited for a freshly grilled hot dog.

"Whom brought the marshmallows?" I asked after dinner. My older sister Carol brought out a bag of marshmallows for toasting. Her and her friends never forget the marshmallows. Them volunteered to toast a marshmallow for everyone.

As the sun set, the mosquitoes came out. It was time to put on bug spray. The adults talked and laughed while the kids kicked a soccer ball. When it was too dark to see, the other kids and me told stories. What a perfect summer day!